Thirteen Turns

Thirteen Turns

A Theology Resurrected From the Gallows
of Jim Crow Christianity

By
LARRY DONELL COVIN JR.

Foreword by
SABRINA L. VALENTE

WIPF & STOCK · Eugene, Oregon

THIRTEEN TURNS
A Theology Resurrected From the Gallows of Jim Crow Christianity

Wipf & Stock
An Imprint of Wipf and Stock Publishers
199 W. 8th Ave., Suite 3
Eugene, OR 97401

www.wipfandstock.com

PAPERBACK ISBN: 978-1-7252-6683-4
HARDCOVER ISBN: 978-1-7252-6684-1
EBOOK ISBN: 978-1-7252-6685-8

Manufactured in the U.S.A.   MAY 27, 2020

Contents

Foreword

WHEN I MET DR. Larry Covin Jr., over a decade ago, I could not have imagined the profound impact he would have on my life. Walking into the correctional facility for the first time, I anticipated my life working with some of the most vulnerable and outcast of our society. I was young, untested, and ready to facilitate meaningful change in the world, one inmate at a time.

It was in this context that I first encountered Dr. Covin, who would introduce me to the work of social justice, in the context of prison reform. Although my tenure working for justice behind the prison walls would be relatively brief, the impact of Dr. Covin's mentoring upon my justice advocacy would be extensive. He has facilitated confidence in me, to the extent that my work with the vulnerable is important, and the professional lessons learned during those experiences, have remained with me as a social justice advocate for the marginalized. I have been protégé, collaborator, and now share an enduring friendship with someone I greatly admire for his work with the vulnerable of our society.

If you will, allow me just a brief moment to introduce myself. I am Sabrina Valente. I earned the bachelor's degree in biblical studies, and a master's degree in forensic psychology. I have spent the last fifteen years working in the mental health field with those that are the most vulnerable in our society. I hold certifications in family trauma and eco-systemic structural family therapy. I have worked in corrections, behavioral health, and suicide prevention. I manage a team of therapists and provide in-home family therapy to those families whose children are at risk for out-of-home placement, who are most often the poor and marginalized. Dr. Covin's work in theology and social justice has served as a blueprint for me in every aspect of my career.

One of the few scholar theologians of color in the United States, Dr. Covin has spent several decades engaged in social justice advocacy, prison system reform, theological education at the graduate level in higher education, public theology, and on the frontlines within the context of the local church. Within the prison reform movement, Dr. Covin has advocated for treatment and rehabilitation, as opposed to punitive measures which have no deterrent effect upon the incarcerated. As an activist theologian, his prophetic proclamations each Sunday from the pulpit of Trinity UCC Church in York, Pennsylvania, challenge systems, public institutions, and destructive thinking concerning race in America.

Dr. Covin has done theology at every level. As a pastoral theologian, as a systematic theologian at the undergraduate and graduate level within higher education, as a director of chaplaincy in the correctional setting, as a director of treatment in the prison system, as a prior service army chaplain, and as an author of public theology.

Dr. Covin holds numerous degrees, including a Bachelor of Science degree in Criminal Justice from Albany State University, Master of Divinity from the Interdenominational Theological Center, Doctor of Ministry degree from the Lancaster Theological Seminary, and a postdoctoral ThM degree in Theology and Ethics from Princeton Theological Seminary.

It was at Princeton Theological Seminary that Dr. Covin was shaped and molded as a systematic theologian; being influenced by the many Princeton Theological Seminary theologians and scholars that have emerged from Princeton. Now, Dr. Covin continues the legacy and tradition of scholarly theological excellence in *Thirteen Turns: A Theology Resurrected From the Gallows of Jim Crow Christianity*.

Thirteen Turns is a much-needed and timely response to the weaponization of Christianity against black and brown bodies. Impacted by the work of James Cone, Jürgen Moltmann, Dietrich Bonhoeffer, Martin Luther King Jr., and other black theology, liberation theology, and pubic theology proponents; *Thirteen Turns* is certain to impact public theology, social justice, and race relations for decades to come.

Written at a time when race and race relations are at the forefront of American lives on a daily basis, at a time when children are separated from parents and caged at our borders, when black and brown men and women are dying at the hands of rogue police officers around the country, when neo-Nazis and white nationalism merge with far-right conservatism, and march the streets with impunity, often under a thinly-veiled guise of the Christian church. *Thirteen Turns* is a theology of hope and resistance. It deconstructs and lays bare the weaponization of religion as an instrument of oppression.

From the very title itself, *Thirteen Turns* demonstrates that Dr. Covin is willing to adopt an iconoclastic approach, to discussing the insidious ways in which Christianity has so often been co-opted and used against people of color, particularly African Americans. *Thirteen Turns* is unflinching and unapologetic in its examination of race and Christianity, and challenges us to authentic and introspective evaluation.

I have no doubt that *Thirteen Turns: A Theology Resurrected From the Gallows of Jim Crow Christianity,* will have a transformative impact upon each reader, as it has very much transformed my thinking about theology and social justice. As you read it, I implore you to stare unflinchingly into the horrors of how a gospel of freedom has been instrumentalized to marginalize our sisters and brothers of color. Stare unflinchingly and internalize the words of Dr. Covin, as he brings to bear the wisdom and insights of not only his research, but of the wisdom of those theologians before him, who hoped and imagined better things to come. Listen to the message of hope and resurrection that is imprinted in each chapter.

Finally, ask yourself, "what am I going to do to bring justice to the world and spaces I occupy?"

With Love for the World,
Sabrina L. Valente, MA, CFTP, CFBMHS

Preface

Thirteen Turns: A Theology Resurrected From the Gallows of Jim Crow Christianity is a response of hope for those who have been victimized by the weaponization of Christianity, either to marginalize persons of color through the legitimizing and sanctioning of Jim Crow, the denial of human rights to Central American refugees at the United States border, or the conflation of nationalism and American exceptionalism with Christianity. Each chapter of *Thirteen Turns* identifies and elucidates the insidious corrupting nature of co-opted Christianity, when it has been instrumentalized to serve nefarious ends.

Thirteen Turns in the literal sense is the number of coils used to construct a hangman's noose. In the United States during the Jim Crow era, the hangman's noose was the ever present symbol of terror and death used for lynching, by some accounts as many as five thousand people. Often, Christianity and its religious leaders, either tacitly and in many cases overtly, sanctioned lynching to enforce vigilante mob violence against African Americans.

The chapters of *Thirteen Turns* were researched and written at Princeton Theological Seminary, as part of a postdoctoral ThM program in Theology and Ethics. Each section was written for a specific research purpose and audience, and documented for the purpose of this book.

The chapters of *Thirteen Turns* are not intended to be sequential; however, each chapter is part of a metanarrative reflecting public theology, liberation theology, black theology, and social justice concerns. Each chapter has its unique focus, yet draws upon and reintroduces theological concepts throughout the book in various contexts. Theological concepts such as imagination, Satan's truth—a concept introduced by Dietrich Bonhoeffer, transvaluation, and other theological constructs reemerge in each chapter in various contexts.

Thirteen Turns: A Theology Resurrected From the Gallows of Jim Crow Christianity is a book concerned with liberation and public theology; however, it is a book for anyone interested in social justice. The research introduced within the pages of *Thirteen Turns* is useful for its sociological value, and will inform those who are students of race relations and justice advocates as well. As such, this book is equally appropriate for the college and university student, seminarian, the local church, as well as those seeking to better understand the intersection of theology, race, and justice in America.

Acknowledgements

I WOULD LIKE TO thank my wife and children for their support and understanding during the research and writing phase of this book. Often, I was away and engaged in my work which took away from significant family time. Gloria Freeman-Covin, Nicholas, Roger, Larry III, and Joel, I cannot thank you enough for your love and patience.

I would be remiss if I did not acknowledge the late Reverend Roger Lee Brown, my grandfather, who was not afforded the opportunity of a high school or college education, yet was the first pastor theologian I was exposed to as a child. Reverend Brown kindled the imagination of this author to aspire to study theology at Princeton Theological Seminary. From the projects to Princeton! Thanks Grandad.

I especially want to thank Princeton Theological Seminary, the very special place Princeton is for engaging theological and scholarly work, the resource of Princeton Theological Seminary Library, as well as the accessibility of many of the leading scholars in the world.

Finally, I want to thank Trinity United Church of Christ in York, Pennsylvania, where I serve as Systematic Theologian and Religion Scholar. The flexibility granted me to travel, research, and write during this period was indispensable and contributed to the completion of *Thirteen Turns*.

Introduction

THIRTEEN TURNS: A THEOLOGY *Resurrected From the Gallows of Jim Crow Christianity* is written from the unique insight of one of the scarcely few theology scholars of color in the United States, who represents a community existentially affected by religion, race, and racism historically and culturally, in a way theologians emerging from the dominant culture are unaffected.

Thirteen Turns introduces, and in some cases reintroduces many of the most significant theologians of Protestantism, to a new generation of those concerned with liberation theology, black theology, public theology, and social justice in our contemporary context.

Theologians and philosophers such as Friedrich Schleiermacher, Reinhold Niebuhr, Howard Thurman, Jürgen Moltmann, James Cone, Dietrich Bonhoeffer, W. E. B. DuBois, Nicholas Wolterstorff, Martin Luther King Jr., Carter G. Woodson, Karl Barth, Bruce McCormack, and many others are introduced into the conversation of race, social justice, and religion in the context of the twenty-first century. In the era of racial profiling and caged children at the borders. In the age of white nationalism and far-right conservatism masquerading as the Christian church.

In much the same way as the German Evangelical Church stood in juxtaposition with the Confessing Church under Bonhoeffer, *Thirteen Turns* elucidates the many insidious religious facades posturing as the Christian church, and its political and civic parastatals.

How to read *Thirteen Turns*—As you read the multifaceted chapters covering diverse topics, there are ten themes which will emerge as a cohesive narrative throughout. The principles are the collective theological ideas of the major theologians in conversation with *Thirteen Turns*. The ten principles emerging in *Thirteen Turns* are:

- *Organic Intellectuals*
- *Satan's Truth*
- *Law and Order*
- *The (class) Room*
- *Imagination*
- *Hope*
- *Transvaluation*
- *Double Consciousness*
- *What Does It Mean To Tell The Truth?*
- *Seeing The Great Events of World History From Below*

What does *Thirteen Turns* have to offer marginalized people in Baltimore, Staten Island, Ferguson, Sanford, Cleveland, and cities around the United States which devalue black and brown lives? An uncovered, reclaimed history of theological hope and resistance, hope and resistance, which sustained generations of Africans, as well as Africans in the diaspora, descents of all "*shithole countries*," through lynching and American domestic terrorism. It offers insights gained from extensive research that stands ready to inform all engaged in justice work on multiple fronts.

CHAPTER 1

The Theology of Friedrich Schleiermacher in Black Religious Thought and Practices

I. Introduction

THIS CHAPTER WILL EXPLORE the phenomenon of *the feeling of absolute dependence* and *God-consciousness, self-consciousness, feeling of freedom, fellowship of believers, blessedness, outer circle of the church, the elect, personal immortality and afterlife*, as well as other theological concepts central to the work of Friedrich Schleiermacher, in the context of the black religious experience encompassing African religious heritage, as well as African American religious expression in the United States.

Historically, marginalized African Americans have articulated their experiences relative to God, in their religious rituals and practices, transcendental to *liberal Christian* experience informed through Enlightenment theologies. More specifically, an exploration of the commonalities and differences between African American religious experience of *feeling of absolute dependence* and *God-consciousness*, inherited by African traditional religious experience and lived experience in America, and the *feeling of absolute dependence* and *God-consciousness* in Schleiermacher's theology will be considered. A significant goal of this chapter is to bring Schleiermacher into conversation with black religious experience, and to demonstrate how Schleiermacher's theology and theological concepts show up in black religious thought and practices.

This author will argue that communities and persons lacking power and franchisement are intrinsically positioned to experience *feeling of absolute dependence* and *God-consciousness*, due to their alienation from societies possessing alternatives to reliance upon religion, religious practices, rituals, and religious instructions. As a result, *the feeling of absolute dependence* and *God-consciousness* for historically marginalized groups is unobstructed.

This *religious state of mind* and *the feeling of absolute dependence* as well as understanding of *God-consciousness* needs to be explored in new contexts, and in ways which brings Schleiermacher into conversation with divergent and emerging religious experiences vis-à-vis black religious experience. As such, this author acknowledges the risk of engaging theological ideas from the eighteen and nineteenth centuries, with very specific religious experience and language inherent in black religion and thought. *The theology of Friedrich Schleiermacher in black religious thought and practices* is an attempt to lessen the divide between the two.

II. Schleiermacher / Thurman / Du Bois / McCormack / Mill / Rousseau / Sartre

The African enslaved in America intrinsically imagined and comprehended a beingness which allowed for self-transcendence, a move which created tension with the dialectic of being enslaved, yet possessing an awareness of the freedom inherent in God. The African enslaved possessed an *intuition of the universe* as Schleiermacher would refer to it as in *On Religion: Speeches to its Cultured Despisers*. "The standard by which all are measured is that of intuitions of the universe. Whether we have a God as a part of our intuition depends on the direction of our imagination . . . since imagination is the highest and most original element in us."[1] The African enslaved clearly possessed a *direction of imagination* that synthesized God into his existence. The African enslaved in America had only religious beliefs to sustain herself in the face of relentless denial of her humanity. "A God who is worthy of our belief must be believed in, not because of his potential beneficence but because of an overwhelming necessity that arises from our experience of the world."[2]

A feeling of *Absolute Dependence* upon God would by necessity diminish the dependence upon the one enslaving the African in America, that is to say the slave owner, and would therefore undermine the premise upon which the institution of slavery is built. It is antithetical to the human experience to not possess agency, or to dispossess a subject of autonomy and/or freedom. Despite the postulation of Jean Jacques Rousseau, writing in *Rousseau's The Social Contract,* stating that eventually persons confined to a certain condition, will accept his or her condition without attempting to improve upon their circumstances; historic documents and accounts of the earnest yearning of the African to experience freedom negates this account. "Slaves lose everything in their chains, even the desire of escaping them . . ."[3]

As a subject, the enslaved African is nevertheless bound by a nature informed by the theological understanding of *imago Dei*, and therefore desires freedom. The rituals and rites found in religious experience facilitate a dependence upon God, a consciousness, as the African understood God; to the extent that his and her self-transcendence could not be contained by either whips, chains or the weaponizing of a pornographic religion as presented by White Christianity. Howard Thurman, writing in *The Creative Encounter* identifies this consciousness or untouchable reality that is resident in all humanity. "As a person each of us lives a private life; there is a world within where for us the great issues of our

1. Schleiermacher, *On Religion*, 65.

2. Schleiermacher, *On Religion*, 65.

3. Rousseau, *The Social Contract*, 6.

lives are determined . . . It is private. It is cut off from immediate involvement in what surrounds us. It is my world."[4]

To be a part of humanity is to desire freedom. It is as *sentient beings* the African enslaved has a consciousness of his or her place, an awareness of freedom even without the experience of freedom. To lack this awareness is to lack being a part of humanity. Writing in *The Christian Faith*, Schleiermacher observes; "This last expression includes the God-consciousness in the self-consciousness in such a way that . . . the two cannot be separated from each other."[5]

This move creates a dialectic for the African enslaved. It is in their self-consciousness that they are awakened to their God-consciousness, and thus their lack of freedom is exacerbated exponentially. The African enslaved consequently realizes the perverted tension between freedom and bondage, self-consciousness and God-consciousness. Despite the dialectic of inherently desiring freedom, and knowing the institution of slavery negated this basic human desire, it is more desirable to yearn for freedom than to not. John Stuart Mill captures this sentiment. "It is better to be a human being dissatisfied than a pig satisfied; better to be Socrates dissatisfied than a fool satisfied. And if the fool, or the pig, are a different opinion, it is because they only know their own side of the question."[6]

How could the African enslaved have experienced so much as an approximation of *flourishing* in the midst of rape, family separation, physical torture, and denial of personality? Schleiermacher's theology of absolute dependence and consciousness is a theological move that may lend insight into the negation of the aforementioned deprivations.

How did the African enslaved maintain, or better yet, achieve that *self identity* described by Schleiermacher, with the outward distraction of the so-called *peculiar institution* of slavery, to achieve the optimum level of consciousness in Schleiermacher's theology, which leads to what Schleiermacher calls *blessedness*? Dr. Bruce

4. Thurman, *The Creative Encounter*, 19.

5. Hodgkin and King, *Readings In Christian Theology*, 157.

6. Mill, *Utilitarianism*.

McCormack of Princeton Theological Seminary, in a lecture titled "Locating Christian Faith on a Map of Religious Consciousness," observes the following. " . . . The feeling of absolute dependence joins itself to differing sets of circumstances . . . we will experience pleasure or pain. . . . Where and when we remain identical with ourselves through these varying conditions, we experience the highest state of consciousness possible, which Schleiermacher calls blessedness."[7]

The African enslaved, according to Schleiermacher's theology pertinent to absolute dependence and consciousness, could have experienced the most extreme dialectic of human deprivation as a slave, while achieving blessedness as a result of his or her consciousness. Revisionist historians have incorrectly characterized the African enslaved in America as being content in their circumstances of captivity. Nothing could be more inaccurate. It can be posited that the African enslaved episodically accomplished a *religious ecstasy* which negated the draconian realities of slavery, thereby facilitating a transcendental experience of which no chain or whip could deny. McCormack observes, "The more the feeling of absolute dependence masters the stimuli that come from without, the more religious she is."[8]

Religion for the African enslaved in America, was simply another medium of communication, to accompany his or her spirituality embraced through their familiarity with African traditional religion, or ATR practices. Thurman observes, "Religious experience is interpreted to mean the conscious and direct exposure of the individual to God."[9]

This inner consciousness was a habitation or retreat for the African enslaved, an untouchable enclave, an impenetrable fortification which emancipated his or her soul from the dehumanizing realities of slavery. Manning Marble writing in *The Meaning of Faith in the Black Mind In Slavery* makes the following observation. "Jean Paul Sartre discussed the existentialist limits of man's

7. McCormack, "Locating Christian Faith."
8. McCormack, "Locating Christian Faith."
9. Thurman, *The Creative Encounter*, 20.

freedom . . . in the oppressive society, the *Other* holds a secret—the secret of what I am . . . Blacks continually found . . . their African culture negated, and their spirituality redefined. During slavery, the Black man sought continually to lay claim, as Sartre suggests, to this being which I am . . ."[10]

In effect, the African had no alternatives available to attach to other than God. Schleiermacher observes, "The common element in all those determinations of self-consciousness . . . is the feeling of dependence . . . the common element in all those determinations . . . is the feeling of freedom."[11]

The theological question is whether a subject can have spiritual freedom while in the throes of bondage and servitude? Do the limitations placed upon the humanity of an individual thereby infringe upon the transcendental realities of the subject? Schleiermacher states, "Accordingly our self-consciousness, as a consciousness of our existence in the world or our co-existence with the world, is a series in which the feeling of freedom and the feeling of dependence are divided."[12]

W. E. B. Du Bois while speaking in a totally different context yet spoke of a divided reality for the African in America. Schleiermacher's discussion of the relationship between freedom and dependence, self-consciousness and God-consciousness, have at times inexplicable moves, that defy demystification; how much the more when considering additional external considerations such as enslavement. How much more elusive for the African in America, to understand a spiritual type of *double consciousness,* in addition to the double consciousness of being bodily immobilized. " . . . In *The Souls of Black Folk* (1903) in which Du Bois spoke of an African American double consciousness, a two-ness of being an American, a Negro; two warring ideals in one dark body, whose dogged strength alone keeps it from being torn asunder."[13]

---

10. Marable, "The Meaning of Faith."

11. Hodgkin and King, *Readings In Christian Theology,* 154.

12. Hodgkin and King, *Readings in Christian Theology,* 155.

13. Du Bois, *Souls of Black Folk,* 236.

Du Bois described a double consciousness of faith and doubt to describe the black religious experience of the African enslaved in America. "Somewhat like his use of the concept of double consciousness . . . Du Bois used the paradox of faith and doubt together . . . One cannot correctly understand the black religious experience without an affirmation of deep faith informed by doubt."[14]

III. Schleiermacher / Bonhoeffer / De La Torre / Cone / King / Hegel / McCormack

The African enslaved in America it may be argued constitutes the true church or the authentic church. The grounds for such a claim is that biblically, historically, or otherwise it has been shown that the church of Christ is a church in tension, a church in opposition to the authorities and magistrates, a church that is persecuted. This is the biblical ideal of the church. The meta-narrative of the suffering church suggests other than flourishing. This would constitute a church representative of oppressed peoples.

In Schleiermacher's theology a strong emphasis is placed upon the role of the fellowship of believers. Schleiermacher in *The Christian Faith* makes this claim: "All that comes to exist in the world through redemption is embraced in the fellowship of believers, within which all regenerate people are always found."[15] That the African enslaved is constituent to the *true church* is a function of being redeemed by Christ. The African enslaved as representative of the *true church* is held in tension with his lack of observable freedom; however, consistent with her being *the suffering church*. "But the truth is that the new life of each individual springs from that of the community, while the life of the community springs from no other individual life than that of the Redeemer. We must therefore hold that the totality of those who live in the state of sanctification is the inner fellowship . . . "[16]

---

14. Cone, *The Cross and the Lynching Tree*, 106.

15. Schleiermacher, *The Christian Faith*, 525.

16. Hodgkin and King, *Readings In Christian Theology*, 248.

Dietrich Bonhoeffer makes the claim that this *inner fellowship* is *the view from below*. Bonhoeffer posits that it is from below that a clarity emerges both to and through the believer, that is obscured outside of this inner fellowship. Clifford J. Green and Michael P. DeJonge in *The Bonhoeffer Reader: Letters and Papers from Prison*, give insight into Bonhoeffer's understanding of the view from below. "It remains an experience of incomparable value that we have for once learned to see the great events of world history from below, from the perspective of the outcasts, the suspects, the maltreated, the powerless, the oppressed and the reviled, in short from the perspective of the suffering."[17] The African enslaved in America qualifies without necessity of much theological imagination. It is in this claim that this author's original argument is grounded; communities and persons lacking power and franchisement, are intrinsically positioned to experience *feeling of absolute dependence* and *God-consciousness*.

Can the argument be made that those who enslaved the African in America are part of the inner fellowship as well, united in Christ with those of whom they enslaved? On what grounds is such an argument made? Miguel A. De La Torre writing in *Doing Christian Ethics from the Margins* renders his perspective. "Conversion for those of the dominant culture moves beyond simple belief . . . conversion moves toward . . . a praxis that breaks with personal and social sin and leads the new believer to . . . begin a new life in Christ manifested as solidarity with the same people Jesus sought to identify himself with, the outcasts."[18]

If the fellowship of believers share the same redemption in the world as Schleiermacher suggests, then the African enslaved as well as the slaveholder are united in this fellowship. It is incongruent then to hold that these subjects are a part of the same fellowship of believers, when taken into consideration the relationship of dominator and dominated. One is a part of the inner fellowship, and one is not a part of the inner fellowship. The one who is suffering in the way that reflects the suffering of Jesus best qualifies as

---

17. Bonhoeffer, *The Bonhoeffer Reader*, 775.

18. De La Torre, *Christian Ethics from the Margins*, 45.

part of the fellowship of believers. W. E. B. Du Bois would answer Schleiermacher in this fashion; "Du Bois elaborated on why the white Christ was not the biblical Christ . . . If Jesus Christ came to America He would associate with Negroes and Italian and working people; He would eat and pray with them, and He would seldom see the interior of the Cathedral of Saint John the Divine."[19]

Schleiermacher's earlier statement, *All that comes to exist in the world through redemption is embraced in the fellowship of believers,* is echoed in the Reverend Dr. Martin Luther King's declaration of the *beloved community.* The failure to embrace the manifestation of this redemption by the fellowship of believers further strengthens the argument that slave owners, segregationists, white nationalists, and other separatists fail to meet the basic criteria of Schleiermacher's claim. "Dr. King's Beloved Community . . . in which all people can share in the wealth of the earth . . . Poverty, hunger and homelessness will not be tolerated because . . . racism . . . bigotry and prejudice will be replaced by an all-inclusive spirit of sisterhood and brotherhood."[20]

The African enslaved in America, and the white abolitionists, are those who most closely experience self-transcendence, and possess sufficient imagination to approximate Schleiermacher's fellowship of believers. "That wherever regenerate persons are within reach of each other, some kind of fellowship between them is bound to arise. For if they are in contact, their witness to the faith must in part overlap, and must necessarily involve mutual recognition and a common understanding as to their operation within the common area."[21] Nothing short of manumission satisfies Schleiermacher's claim.

In a move which seeks to not dispense of those who claim affiliation with the church, yet who are complicit in the institution of slavery, and participate in the dehumanizing practices which negate personality and flourishing, Schleiermacher refers to this category as the *outer circle* of the Church. Bruce McCormack,

19. Cone, *The Cross and the Lynching Tree,* 103.

20. The King Center, "The King Philosophy."

21. Hodgkin and King, *Readings In Christian Theology,* 248.

in a lecture titled "The Origin of the Church: Election and the Communication of the Holy Spirit," illuminates Schleiermacher's understanding of the outer circle. "But there are also to be found those who are attracted to the fellowship, those who wish to associate themselves with it . . . Such people do not participate as yet in the power of Jesus' God Consciousness or His blessedness . . . Schleiermacher refers to this group as the outer circle . . ."[22]

There is a sense, long in the making within the marginalized community, that the oppressed play a role in the redemption of the oppressor. The Reverend Dr. Martin Luther King Jr. captures this sentiment and is recalled in an article titled, "Address at the Conclusion of the Selma to Montgomery March." "But not until the colossus of segregation was challenged in Birmingham did the conscience of America begin to bleed. White America was profoundly aroused by Birmingham because it witnessed the whole community of Negroes facing terror and brutality with majestic scorn and heroic courage."[23]

The philosopher Hegel postulates that the oppressor is ensnared in the very diabolical circumstances of which he creates. "German philosopher Hegel's concept of 'Lordship and Bondage,' as found in his *The Phenomenology of Mind*, avers that the master (the oppressor) is also subjected to the structures he creates to enslave the laborer (1967:238–40). Because oppressive structures also prevent the master from obtaining an abundant life . . ."[24]

Schleiermacher refers to the regenerate as the *elect*. Arguably, the elect comprised the African enslaved in America, *the Crucified People* as Jon Sobrino refers to them as, the people Mark Twain referred to in his 1901 essay "The United States of Lyncherdom," and the elect chronicled in James Cone's *The Cross and the Lynching Tree*. The idea that *unmerited suffering is redemptive,* and the proposition that *suffering is salvific,* have fallen out of use in many theological circles. Perhaps the inexplicable suffering encountered

22. McCormack, "The Origin of the Church."

23. King Jr., "Address at the Conclusion of the Selma to Montgomery March," para. 5.

24. De La Torre, *Christian Ethics from the Margins*, 16–17.

by the African enslaved, is a transvaluation of the nonsensical element of suffering. Could it be that the only redeemable aspect of suffering in this concern is to bring those in the outer circle closer to the elect? "They are those who are being called but whose calling has yet to reach its goal in them. Those who are truly regenerate . . . constitute the inner circle. They alone have experienced redemption . . . they are the elect."[25]

IV. Schleiermacher / Achebe

Personal immortality of believers is for Schleiermacher a significant break with the African enslaved, and his religious imagination pertinent to the afterlife. Schleiermacher wrote in his *Addresses on Religion* that the desire for an afterlife is decidedly not a demonstration of strong religious belief. "Believe in God, and in personal immortality, are not necessarily a part of religion . . . the desire for personal immortality seems rather to show a lack of religion, since religion assumes a desire to lose oneself in the infinite . . ."[26] Schleiermacher seems to posit the desire for Christian afterlife as a type of egoism or anthropocentrism, something that removes the focus away from God and is tethered to self-preservation.

For the African enslaved, the afterlife was the only semblance of flourishing he could imagine through self-transcendence, and thus a move indispensable to the African's faith or belief system. Chinua Achebe illuminates the importance of the afterlife for the African in her faith traditions. Writing in *Things Fall Apart* Achebe makes the following observation. "Igbo speaking people of Southeast Nigeria believed that the ancestral spirits and the spiritual world in which they lived were directly linked to the world of the living. They believed that death was not the end of the spirit's journey . . ."[27]

25. McCormack, "The Origin of the Church."

26. Kedourie, *Nationalism*.

27. Achebe, *Things Fall Apart*, 122.

The God-consciousness, so foundational to the theology of Schleiermacher, shows up in a nuanced form in African traditional religion in general and Yoruba belief systems in particular. J. Omosade Awolalu writing in *Yoruba Beliefs and Sacrificial Rites* makes the following observation: "In spite of the varied forms and systems, religious consciousness permeates every portion of African life; secularity has no reality in the African existence . . . contemporary African scholars believe that generally all people and groups of Africa believe in a supreme, self-existent deity.[28]

This consciousness was part of the formation the African enslaved in America transported with him to the new world. Many African scholars believe that Christianity was an adaptation of the religious consciousness, permeating African traditional religious beliefs, and was coterminous with the emerging spirituality of the African in Africa and America. "Furthermore, for many of the slaves who practiced traditional African religions prior to arriving on Southern plantations, Christianity elucidated their theology because it was fastened to a set of theological convictions and practices that already fit their existing presuppositions.[29]

V. Schleiermacher / Mitchell

The contemporary black religious experience is a continuation of the God-consciousness prevalent in African traditional religion and the African enslaved in America. Henry H. Mitchell chronicles this reality in *Black Belief: Folk Beliefs of Blacks in America and West Africa*. "In recent years, historian Henry H. Mitchell argues in his book . . . that Du Bois was correct in his assertion. Black faith in America today, as he states, is a carryover from traditional African religions."[30]

So completely synthesized into the black experience in the United States is the God-consciousness, that even so-called secular

---

28. Grant, "Ancient African Religion," para. 21.

29. Grant, "Ancient African Religion," para. 5.

30. Grant, "Ancient African Religion," para. 17.

venues exhibit elements of black religious conscience. In an article titled *Jazz: A Multicultural Phenomenon* by Bruce Mitchell this influence is on full display. "Strongly influenced by the music of the black church and the miseries of slavery, the blues was another of the building blocks of American jazz. Blues singers . . . were prominent black contributors to this American art form . . . "[31]

The ubiquity of God-consciousness in black culture manifests in the ability to *code switch* with relative ease, from rhythmic dance in celebratory Saturday evening convenings, to Sunday church worship experiences. The seamless movement between the two realities recalls the aforementioned, that there is no construct of the separation of the sacred and the secular in the African idiom. This phenomenon is a direct inheritance of the African influence on black religious experience and expression. God-consciousness is all pervasive.

Finally, Friedrich Schleiermacher provides language that is useful in thinking about black religious thought and practices, outside of traditional black theology and liberation theology; such as the feeling of absolute dependence and God-consciousness, self-consciousness, feeling of freedom, fellowship of believers, blessedness, outer circle of the church, the elect, and personal immortality and afterlife. All of which are prominent in black religious thought and practices, and hopefully illuminated to a greater extent in this chapter.

31. Mitchell, "Jazz: A Multicultural Phenomenon," 236–38.

CHAPTER 2

Beyond Vietnam

A Time to Break Silence in Conversation with
A Theological Perspective From The Margins

Note: Dr. Covin is a Prior Service Army Commissioned Officer and Paratrooper

THE REVEREND DR. MARTIN Luther King Jr. in an arguably un-precedented display of moral, ethical, and theological autonomy, spoke out against a sitting United States president; Lyndon Baines Johnson in opposition to the war in Vietnam on April 4, 1967, at The Riverside Church in New York. Against the advice of both supporters and critics, Dr. King decidedly interjected himself into the foray of foreign affairs, in juxtaposition to his civil rights agenda concerned with the domestic policies of Jim Crow segregation and oppression.

King posited, that by speaking out against the war in Vietnam, he was supporting civil rights at home. Writing in *A Testament of Hope: The Essential Writings of Marin Luther King Jr.*, James M. Washington captures the prophetic voice of King. "There is at the outset a very obvious and almost facile connection between the war in Vietnam and the struggle, I, and others, have been waging in America. A few years ago . . . it seemed as if there was a real promise of hope for the poor . . . through the poverty program."[1]

The poverty program would culminate in the so-called *Poor People's Campaign,* in which the primary tenets of generational poverty would be illuminated and elucidated in order to redress their causes. Dr. King felt the war in Vietnam negated the progress their efforts had garnered to date. "There were experiments, hopes, new beginnings. Then came the buildup in Vietnam and I watched the program broken and eviscerated as if it were some ideal political plaything of a society gone mad on war . . . "[2]

The dichotomy of civil rights and foreign policy is a false construct. Dr. King effectively demonstrates the inextricable relationship between foreign policy, domestic policy, and civil rights.

War has many deleterious effects upon a nation and its citizenry. At times, war is instrumentalized to rally around nationalism, to export the misguided philosophy of American exceptionalism, or to create inroads for capitalism and exploitation of land and resources abroad. "With righteous indignation, it will look across the seas and see individual capitalists of the West investing huge sums of money in Asia, Africa and South America, only to take the profits out with no concern for the social betterment of the countries, and say: This is not just . . . "[3]

Dr. King found the war in Vietnam objectionable on many levels. Central to the civil rights movement, however, was its exploitation of the poor. Some economist estimates put the total cost of the Vietnam War at billions of dollars. " . . . America would never invest the necessary funds or energies in rehabilitation of its poor so long as adventures like Vietnam continued to draw men and skills and money like some demonic destructive suction tube. So I was increasingly compelled to see the war as an enemy of the poor and to attack it as such."[4]

---

1. King Jr., *A Testament of Hope,* 232.
2. King Jr., *A Testament of Hope,* 232.
3. King Jr., *A Testament of Hope,* 241.
4. King Jr., *A Testament of Hope,* 233.

The Vietnam War, like wars in general, tends to encapsulate the worst tendencies found within human nature. The propensity to exploit power against weakness. The impulse to hoard resources for the rich at the expense of the poor. What Dr. King lifted his voice against in the context of the Vietnam War was simply a reiteration of the human inclination toward egoism. King was therefore engaged in opposition to human nature manifest in his generation within the context of the Vietnam War.

Reinhold Niebuhr writing in *Moral Man And Immoral Society* captures this tension. "Though human society has roots which lie deeper in history than the beginning of human life, men have made comparatively but little progress in solving the problem of their aggregate existence."[5]

The so-called *American original sin* of white oppression of black people vis-à-vis the institution of slavery, is yet another manifestation of this failure to cohabitate. "Each century originates a new complexity and each new generation faces a new vexation in it. For all the centuries of experience, men have not yet learned how to live together without impounding their vices and covering each other with mud and with blood."[6]

The Vietnam War was yet another opportunity for the wealthy, the powerful, and the political elites of the United States, to exploit the most vulnerable within their borders. Black men, predominantly poor and undereducated, were enlisted disproportionately to white men to engage the war effort in Vietnam. This discrepancy was particularly offensive and hypocritical to King. "It was sending their sons and their brothers and their husbands to fight and to die in extraordinarily high proportions relative to the rest of the population."[7]

Heretofore, America had little use for black masculinity, often reflected in the staggering numbers of black youth unemployed, ensnared in the criminal justice system, or victims of drug infested ghettos of New York, Detroit, and Chicago. The war in Vietnam

5. Niebuhr, *Moral Man*, 1.

6. Niebuhr, *Moral Man*, 1.

7. King Jr., *A Testament of Hope*, 233.

and their conscription created a need for black bodies. "We were taking the black young men who have been crippled by our society and sending them eight thousand miles away to guarantee liberties in Southeast Asia which they had not found in southwest Georgia and East Harlem."[8]

The phenomenon of making use of the most vulnerable, the least politically engaged, and those living in the margins, dates to circa AD 120 and captured in the words of Plutarch to Tiberius Gracchus. " . . . Powerful classes enlist their slaves in the defense of their dominions. . . . The poor folk go to war, to fight and to die for the delights, riches and superfluities of others. In the long run these pretensions are revealed and the sentiment of patriotism is throttled in the breasts of the disinherited."[9] Dr. King suggested that it was only a matter of time before the poor black soldiers fighting in Vietnam understood the magnitude of the deception of its government, the propagandizing of the war under the guise of patriotism, much like the slaves referenced by Plutarch. "We are adding cynicism to the process of death, for they must know after a short period there that none of the things we claim to be fighting for are really involved. . . . The more sophisticated surely realize that we are on the side of the wealthy and the secure while we create a hell for the poor."[10]

A familiar strategy of the powerful is to wrap the conversation in the flag of patriotism. Those who challenge the reasoning of the call-to-war connection with patriotism endure social criticism, imprisonment, ostracism or worse. Muhammad Ali understood, prior to most during the pinnacle of the Vietnam War, the fallacious annexing of serving in Vietnam with patriotism.

The powerful of our society often use their power to achieve their ends. Niebuhr refers to this misuse of power as *types and combinations* of power. Writing in *The Nature And Destiny Of Man II* Niebuhr makes the following observation. "The spiritual and physical faculties of man are able, in their unity and interrelation,

---

8. King Jr., *A Testament of Hope*, 233.

9. Niebuhr, *Moral Man*, 11.

10. King Jr., *A Testament of Hope*, 238.

to create an endless variety of types and combinations of power, from that of pure reason to that of pure physical force."[11]

The power in this instance is to create a sentiment of nationalism cloaked in patriotism in support of the Vietnam War. "Though reason is commonly supposed to be transcendent, rather than partial, it is hardly necessary at this point to prove that reason may be the instrument of the ego in advancing its claims against another. When it is so used it is a power which supports the claims of one life against another."[12]

Dr. King claimed that his commitment to Jesus Christ was a calling to a higher allegiance than to nationalism. This declaration runs counter to the conflation of religion with nationalism, Christianity with Western assumptions and values, and capitalism with Protestantism. " . . . And I cannot forget that the Nobel Prize for Peace was also a commission—a commission to work harder than I had ever worked before the brotherhood of man [sic]. This is a calling that takes me beyond national allegiances . . . "[13]

Dr. King clearly understood the concept of *organic intellectuals* as espoused by Miguel A. De La Torre, and embraced by many theologians originating in communities of color and oppression. " . . . Ministers and scholars attempt to learn from the disenfranchised while serving them as organic intellectuals (to borrow a term from Antonio Gramsci), that is, intellectuals grounded in the social reality of the marginalized, and acting in the consciousness-raising process of the faith community."[14]

One of the significant critiques King makes of America is its feeling of superiority, arrogance, and paternalism on the world stage. One contributing factor for this phenomenon is due to political leaders making decisions untethered from the experiences of people in the margins, unlike organic intellectuals who ground their practices in the context of the lived experiences of the people. "The Western arrogance of feeling that it has everything to teach

11. Niebuhr, *Nature and Destiny*, 270.

12. Niebuhr, *Nature and Destiny*, 270.

13. King Jr., *A Testament of Hope*, 234.

14. De La Torre, *Christian Ethics from the Margins*, xii.

others and nothing to learn from them is not just . . . "[15] This feeling of arrogance played out in American foreign policy toward Vietnam then, as it plays out now on the world stage. "The Vietnamese people proclaimed their own independence in 1945 . . . our government felt then that the Vietnamese people were not ready for independence, and we again fell victim to the deadly Western arrogance that has poisoned the international atmosphere for so long."[16]

In the historic speech "Beyond Vietnam," a watershed moment in Dr. King's commentary upon American foreign affairs, King offered that the wisdom of those who are the most vulnerable in society may have the most insight pertinent to coexistence within the social contract, as well as their *revelation of God* to borrow from Karl Barth. " . . . To see the enemy's point of view . . . from his view we may indeed see the basic weaknesses of our own condition . . . we may learn and grow and profit from the wisdom of the brothers who are called the opposition."[17]

Dietrich Bonhoeffer, confined to a German Nazi prison cell, came to understand the perspective of those marginalized, that there is a clarity of *God-consciousness*, to borrow from Schleiermacher, that is absent from those wielding power. Writing in *The View from Below* Bonhoeffer states this with marked clarity. "It remains an experience of incomparable value that we have for once learned to see the great events of world history from below, from the perspective of the outcasts . . . in short from the perspective of the suffering . . . that we come to see . . . clearer, freer, more incorruptible . . . "[18] King and Bonhoeffer would agree that the Vietnamese people have something to offer the world, humanity, and those who manipulate the *levers of power.*

The Vietnam War served many purposes for the American government. King, as does this author, suggests that one purpose Vietnam served is as a laboratory for experimentation. Much like

15. King Jr., *A Testament of Hope*, 241.

16. King Jr., *A Testament of Hope*, 235.

17. King Jr., *A Testament of Hope*, 237.

18. Bonhoeffer, *The Bonhoeffer Reader*, 775.

the lessons learned in weaponry and warfare by dropping the atomic bomb on Hiroshima and Nagasaki, America has used its military, economic, and political might in experiments upon the vulnerable and people of color around the world. "What do they think as we test our latest weapons on them, just as the Germans tested out new medicine and new tortures in the concentration camps of Europe?"[19]

Reinhold Niebuhr postulates that with the disproportionately of power comes a negation of justice. The advances in human ingenuity have the potential to create human flourishing; however, the advances made in technology are often used to serve nefarious human endeavor. Niebuhr observes this dialectic. "The same technology, which drew the fangs of nature's enmity of man, also created a society in which the intensity and extent of social cohesion has been greatly increased, and in which power is so unevenly distributed . . . "[20]

Perhaps it can be argued, the downfall of many communities of color vis-à-vis Vietnam and other brown countries is that they either lack technology rivaling the West, or they have chosen underdevelopment as a minimalist way of life. This leaves them vulnerable to predatory nations which only value military might and expansion. The inequities of power are the necessary antecedents to injustice around the world and domestically. ". . . That justice has become a more difficult achievement. Perhaps it is man's sorry fate, suffering from ills which have their source in the inadequacies of both nature and human society, that the tools by which he eliminates the former should become the means of increasing the latter."[21]

Injustice is not simply an abstraction. Injustice loses its potency in statistics alone. The power of a Dr. King is the ability to repurpose abstractions into imagery in the imagination of the listener in the United States. It is the disturbing images emanating from "Beyond Vietnam A Time to Break Silence" that drew

19. King Jr., *A Testament of Hope*, 236.
20. Niebuhr, *Moral Man*, 2.
21. Niebuhr, *Moral Man*, 2.

the ire of the American government. The sanitized depiction of the war across television screens was disrupted by King's portrayal of the war. "So far we may have killed a million of them—mostly children. They wander . . . homeless, without clothes, running in packs on the streets like animals . . . degraded by our soldiers as they beg for food . . . selling their sisters to our soldiers, soliciting for their mothers."[22]

Confronted with the realities of the Vietnam War, Grenada Invasion, Operation Desert Shield, Second Persian Gulf War, Abu Ghraib Prisoner Torture; America disassociates its role in the global hostilities displayed against it. And yet, in a type of spiritual and religious dissonance, Americans did and do now, weep at the playing of the National Anthem during entertainment sporting events, conflate Christianity with nationalism, and tout our brand of theocratic Americana around the world. As we call ourselves a Christian nation, yet we display violence before the world. "I knew that I could never again raise my voice against the violence of the oppressed in the ghettos without having first spoken clearly to the greatest purveyor of violence in the world today—my own government."[23]

Howard Thurman in *Jesus And The Disinherited* mused pensively concerning the seeming inability of Christianity to serve as a corrective to this glaring contradiction. " . . . Christianity seems impotent to deal radically, and therefore effectively, with the issues of discrimination and injustice on the basis of race, religion and national origin? Is this impotency due to a betrayal of the genius of the religion, or is it due to a basic weakness in the religion itself."[24]

Martin Luther King Jr. lived out the prophetic decree of the biblical text mandating justice for all of God's creation. He took seriously the call to justice for the *least of these* in his challenge to the Vietnam War. Justice for King meant real action and not symbolic gestures of goodwill. "The Old Testament declarations about justice is the passionate insistence that all the members of

22. King Jr., *A Testament of Hope*, 236.

23. King Jr., *A Testament of Hope*, 233.

24. Thurman, *Jesus and the Disinherited*, 7.

the community are entitled to a full and secure place in the life of the community. Hence the clanging repetitive reference to orphans, widows and sojourner."[25]

Dr. King audaciously integrated civil rights with foreign policy. As such, he would no longer be the leader of a domestic civil rights movement in America, leading primarily African Americans in the struggle against injustice and oppression. As a leading voice on American foreign policy vis-à-vis the Vietnam War, King would now purportedly be the leader of white America as well. This placed King in the dubious position of emerging from the designated caste of the Negro in America. If America could tolerate a prominent, world-renowned African American leading the Civil Rights movement, it could not accept an African American encroaching upon the holy grail of American government. One year from the date of King's "Beyond Vietnam" speech he was assassinated in Memphis, Tennessee.

25. Wolterstorff, *Educating for Shalom*, 143.

CHAPTER 3

Nicholas Wolterstorff on Faith and Public Life Together

Justice and Rights in Conversation with a Theological Perspective from Below

I. Introduction

THEOLOGICAL PERSPECTIVES INFORMED BY *organic intellectuals,* or those informed and shaped through encounters with marginalized communities, will serve as the grounds for understanding a largely underrepresented perspective pertaining to justice and rights. " . . . Ministers and scholars attempt to learn from the disenfranchised while serving them as organic intellectuals (to borrow a term from Antonio Gramsci), that is, intellectuals grounded in the social reality of the marginalized . . . "[1] It is within this aforementioned context that Nicholas Wolterstorff's *Faith and Public Life Together: Justice and Rights* will be engaged in conversation with perspectives from John Rawls, Howard Thurman, Reinhold Niebuhr, Dietrich Bonhoeffer, Miguel A. De La Torre,

1. De La Torre, *Christian Ethics from the Margins*, xii.

Jean-Jacques Rousseau, Martin Luther King Jr., Amitabh Chandra of the Harvard Kennedy School, and James H. Cone. More specifically, that arguments concerning justice and rights are legitimized when informed not through untethered abstract constructs, but through experiential realities grounded in marginalized praxis. It is this understanding of justice and rights that serve to provide an ethical and theological perspective from below.

II. Nicholas Wolterstorff / John Rawls / Howard Thurman / Reinhold Niebuhr

Biblical Old Testament scholars often ground their understanding of justice and rights in the context of full franchisement of its citizenry. Justice and rights are assessed relative to how the marginalized are incorporated into full participation within the social contract. Writing in *Educating for Shalom: Essays on Christian Higher Education*, Nicholas Wolterstorff specifies the most vulnerable as participants in justice. "The Old Testament declarations about justice is the passionate insistence that all the members of the community are entitled to a full and secure place in the life of the community. Hence the clanging repetitive reference to orphans, widows and sojourner."[2]

Justice and rights for John Rawls is the equal access to the resources of liberty, social and economic prospects within a society. Historically, even upon the *de jure* reality of the codification of laws intended to achieve a level of parity for all participants, the *de facto* conditions of discrimination and practices furthered the marginalization of the poor in general, and persons of color in particular. Rawls, in his *Two Principles of Justice*, outlines his conception of rights and what individuals should expect from a society concerned with justice and rights. " . . . Right to the most extensive scheme of equal basic liberties compatible with a similar scheme of liberties for others. Social and economic inequalities . . . are both reasonably expected to be to everyone's advantage, and

2. Wolterstorff, *Educating for Shalom*, 143.

attached to positions and offices open to all."[3] Rawls' conception of justice and rights hinges on the ethic of fairness. It is not a welfare state in the popular sense of the definition; however, it suggests that each subject within a society should expect equal opportunities.

That society should be constructed with the telos of justice and rights, Rawls envisions a just society with structures instituting what he refers to as a *veil of ignorance*. "First of all, no one knows his place in society, his class position or social status; nor does he know his fortune in the distribution of natural assets and abilities, his intelligence and strength, and the like."[4] Such an approach to a society comprised of justice and rights would create a society that is concerned with and sensitive to the least capable within a given society, equipping him or her with the instruments to achieve a baseline human dignity common to all participants in a given society, assuming that the architect of such a society may in fact be the *least of these* him or herself.

Christianity provides a move that facilitates human flourishing, justice, and rights. Howard Thurman, writing in *Jesus And The Disinherited*, observes the following. "The religion of Jesus makes the love-ethic central. This is no ordinary achievement. It seems clear that Jesus started out with the simple teaching concerning love embodied in the timeless words of Israel . . . "[5] Here, Jesus makes love of neighbor compulsory to living into Christian community. This move synthesizes justice and rights with love; the three in Jesus' theology and ethics are inextricably fused. "Hear, O Israel: The Lord our God is one Lord: and thou shalt love the Lord thy God with all thy heart, and with all thy soul, and with all thy might, and thy neighbor as thyself. Once the neighbor is defined, then one's moral obligation is clear."[6] Despite the clarity of Jesus' love ethic, many within religious contexts refute the ethics of justice and rights, arguing that such is beyond the scope of religion.

3. Rawls, *A Theory of Justice*, 53.

4. Rawls, *A Theory of Justice*, 118.

5. Thurman, *Jesus and the Disinherited*, 89.

6. Thurman, *Jesus and the Disinherited*, 89.

However, Reinhold Niebuhr postulates that the *moral dimension of sin* negates the imperative Howard Thurman references in Jesus' love ethic. It is this dimension that negates justice and rights of individuals. "But sin also has a moral dimension. The ego which falsely makes itself the center of existence in its pride and will-to-power inevitably subordinates other life to its will. If perfect love is the sacrifice of self, sin is the assertion of self against others . . . "[7]

It is this moral dimension which informs white supremacy and other forms of discrimination, to include policies and laws which value some lives more than others, vis-à-vis President Donald Trump's alleged reference to African countries as "shit-hole" countries, as well as immigration policies that treat immigrants with less than justice and rights. " . . . Sin is always trying to be strong at the expense of someone else. The moral dimension of sin, therefore, is injustice—an unwillingness to value the claims of the other or to see one's own claims as equal but not superior to the other's."[8]

This moral dimension has tangible qualities and influence in the existential and ontological being of its subjects; it deprives people of personality and beingness. "The root of injustice is exploitation, enslaving, or taking advantage of other life."[9]

III. Nicholas Wolterstorff / Dietrich Bonhoeffer / Miguel A. De La Torre

In *Journey Toward Justice,* Nicholas Wolterstorff informs us that not all agree on the concept of justice and rights, and that detractors attempt to steer the conversation away from justice and rights, and to redirect the focus to law and order. "But often defenders of the status quo have found the whole discourse of rights menacing; so, rather than contesting the claims being made for rights, they

7. Lebacqz, *Six Theories of Justice,* 84.
8. Lebacqz, *Six Theories of Justice,* 85.
9. Lebacqz, *Six Theories of Justice,* 85.

have tried to change the terms of the debate . . . let's talk about what's necessary for a well-ordered society."[10]

One of the contrived pseudo-ethical paradigms evil states and governments often establish is under the guise of law and order. It is under such law and order pseudo-ethical paradigms that the apartheid system in South Africa maintained support around the world. It is the same pseudo-ethical paradigm of law and order that facilitated Jim Crow laws, and allowed them to endure for so long because of its disguise of law and order.

It is the same disguise that Hanna Arendt referred to as the *banality of evil*. Writing in *Eichmann in Jerusalem: A Report of the Banality of Evil* Arendt observed the following. "Arendt found Eichmann an ordinary, rather bland, bureaucrat, who in her words, was neither perverted nor sadistic, but terrifyingly normal . . . Instead, he performed evil deeds without evil intentions, a fact connected to his thoughtlessness, a disengagement from the reality of his evil acts."[11] Adolf Eichmann was simply following orders, a claim that has found resonance with law and order adherents.

It is here that Dietrich Bonhoeffer's ethics help to remove the veil and to expose the lie of law and order in its worst context. Clifford Green and Michael DeJonge observe in *The Bonhoeffer Reader* what Bonhoeffer refers to as *Satan's truth*. "There is a such thing as Satan's truth. Its nature is to deny everything real under the guise of the truth. It feeds on hatred against the real, against the world created and loved by God . . . Satan's truth judges what is created out of envy and hatred."[12]

Those who would deny justice and rights to individuals and communities are adept at manipulating their arguments in order to marginalize people ostensibly for law and order. Historically, those who would deny justice and rights to groups of people are tethered to causes which reveal their true intentions, groups such as Breitbart News Network, which cloaks its nationalist ideology behind a thinly veiled pseudo news agency. There are times when

10. Wolterstorff, *Journey Toward Justice*, 37–38.

11. White, "What Did Hannah Arendt Really Mean?," para 2.

12. Bonhoeffer, *The Bonhoeffer Reader*, 754.

the lie is not in the spoken words, however, in the constitution of the person itself. Bonhoeffer states, "These reflections lead to the recognition that the essence of lying is found much deeper than in the contradiction between thought and speech. We could say that the person who stands behind what is said makes it into a lie or the truth."[13]

When Wolterstorff discusses those who promote a well-ordered society over justice and rights, it speaks to the complexity of systems which distort ethics, truth, justice, and rights. Writing in *Doing Christian Ethics from the Margins*, Miguel A. De La Torre observes that structures established by the powerful in society, often under the guise of a well-ordered society, diminish the personality of individuals attempting to adhere to a distorted ethical system, and negate flourishing. De La Torre explains how his mother, an immigrant with no work experience neither the ability to speak English, negotiated laws in place that would potentially shut her out of the workplace. "If she demonstrated the virtue of honesty . . . she would never have been hired. Yet, the moral reasoning she employed enabled her to surmount societal structures fundamentally averse to her very existence. Which is more ethical . . . doing what needs to be done to get the job, or letting the sins of others force us to live on the street?"[14]

A well-ordered society invariably exists to accommodate the powerful in our society. History has demonstrated time and again that law and order, well-ordered societies, negate human flourishing when it comes to the poor and people of color.

IV. Nicholas Wolterstorff / Ulpian / Jean-Jacques Rousseau / Martin Luther King Jr.

Those who oppose the granting of justice and rights do so under the argument of entitlement. The argument is posited in such a way as to suggest that those who argue for justice and rights do

---

13. Bonhoeffer, *The Bonhoeffer Reader*, 754.
14. De La Torre, *Christian Ethics from the Margins*, 22.

so to the detriment of others in the social contract. "The use of rights-talk demotes the giving self and promotes the grasping self, demotes the humble self and promotes the haughty self . . . It invites us to think of ourselves as sovereign individuals."[15] It is presupposed that subjects seeking justice and rights somehow negate the justice and rights of others due to their placing themselves as the focus of a type of just deserts, an individual anthropocentrism which distorts and neglects the attention of others. This type of specious argument is misplaced due to the fact that it assumes that the rewarding one of rights is the negation of the other's rights. "It's made to order for an entitlement society such as ours . . . so it is said, one places oneself at the center of the moral universe, focusing on one's own entitlements to the neglect of one's obligations and to the cultivation of those virtues directed toward others . . . "[16]

This position reverberates in the ongoing debate over affirmative action in higher education today. Again, it is possible to witness the measurable implications of arguments centering around entitlement. Justice and rights in all spheres of our society are framed in the context of who is receiving justice and rights, and whose justice and rights are receding. "Christopher L. Eisgruber, president of Princeton University, used his State of the University letter . . . to respond. I wish, as do many others, that as we search for merit and talent, we no longer had any need to take race into account . . . "[17] President Eisgruber of Princeton University demonstrates an adroitness in his recognition that simply wishing for an egalitarian society, and acting in a way that an egalitarian society already exists, is to deny the reality of the facts of our society. Those who protest justice and rights under the guise of the entitlement argument dismiss the empirical data suggesting parity in our society is far removed from our present reality. President Eisgruber goes on to make the case for justice and rights in higher education. "I instead hoped . . . that our country would act quickly to . . . eliminate racial inequalities in schooling, in policing, in

---

15. Wolterstorff, *Journey Toward Justice*, 38–39.

16. Wolterstorff, *Journey Toward Justice*, 38–39.

17. Jaschik, "Closing Arguments in the Harvard Case," para 9.

health care, in housing and in employment. Had America done so, we would not need to consider race today . . . essential to Princeton's teaching and research mission."[18]

How then do we determine what is justice and what rights pertain to each individual? One idea, or formula, Wolterstorff suggests is that of the Roman Ulpian in the concept known as *ius*. "A well-known formula for justice handed down to us from antiquity comes from the ancient Roman jurist Ulpian: justice, said Ulpian, is rendering to each his or her *ius*-that is, his or her right, his or her due."[19] There are rights due to individuals consequential to their citizenship as part of the state. Yet other rights due may derive as a result of being a sentient being. "Ulpian's formula is a definition of just action: to act justly is to render to each his or her right. Justice characterizes our relationships when we render to others what is their right."[20]

Wolterstorff makes the following observation concerning what he refers to as claim-right. "The life-goods to which one has a claim-right are always ways of being treated. Normally it's to the good of being treated a certain way by others . . . and say that that to which one has a claim-right is always some way of being treated by others that would be a good in one's life."[21]

However, often in the case of marginalized groups, such as African Americans, historically the conduct of the dominant group through their actions causing a *scarcity of resources* has been the wrong. Jean-Jacques Rousseau writing in *The Social Contract and The Discourses* articulates this idea. "The first person who, having enclosed a plot of land, took it unto his head to say this is mine and found people simple enough to believe him was the true founder of civil society."[22] One of the great tragedies, and miscarriages of justice and rights was the removal of Native Americans from their ancestral lands. In the case of African Americans, forced labor was

18. Jaschik, "Closing Arguments in the Harvard Case," para 10.

19. Wolterstorff, *Journey Toward Justice*, 42.

20. Wolterstorff, *Journey Toward Justice*, 42.

21. Wolterstorff, *Journey Toward Justice*, 43–44.

22. Rousseau, *The Social Contract*, 1.

used to cultivate much of the agriculture of the United States, and not able to enjoy the very land they tilled. This is the forfeiture of justice and rights. In a twist of irony, many African Americans fled dehumanizing conditions in the agricultural south for *urban jungles* in the so-called *Great Migration* circa 1916, and lasting some fifty years, displacing them in urban squalor teeming with violence in high-rise tenements within Detroit, Chicago, and other northern cities. The negation of justice and rights of the African American, as well as the Native American, was a result of hoarding land—a resource that existed in abundance. "What crimes, wars, murders, what miseries and horrors would the human race have been spared, had some one pulled up the stakes or filled in the ditch and cried out to his fellow men: Do not listen to this imposter. You are lost if you forget that the fruits of the earth belong to all and the earth to no one!"[23]

In 1896, the United States Supreme Court ruled that it was legal for public entities in the United States to legally impose segregation laws, thereby restricting "Negroes'" access to public facilities. The public segregation of black people and white people further exasperated the sense of second-class citizenry among the Negro population, deepening what W. E. B. Du Bois famously referred to as the *double consciousness effect*. Wolterstorff uses the language *permission-right* to describe the right to do something, as opposed to a right way of being treated. "Our use of the language of rights rather often conceals from us the fact that claim-rights are legitimate claims to ways of being treated. I have a right to walk on the Charlottesville Mall. My walking . . . is not a way of being treated . . . it's something I do . . . I have permission-right . . ."[24]

The Reverend Dr. Martin Luther King Jr. chronicled the effect of segregation and the resulting double consciousness in *Letter From Birmingham City Jail* in 1963, as he articulated the impact of segregation upon his own family. In effect, Dr. King was expressing a negation of permission-rights. " . . . Explain to your six-year old daughter why she can't go to the public amusement park . . . and

23. Rousseau, *The Social Contract*, 1.

24. Wolterstorff, *Journey Toward Justice*, 44.

see the depressing clouds of inferiority begin to form in her little mental sky, and see her begin to distort her little personality."[25]

V. Nicholas Wolterstorff / Amitabh Chandra / James H. Cone

Wolterstorff claims that *rights are normative social relationships*, to use his language. He suggests that rights tacitly imply that rights exist in relationship to the other. " . . . Rights are normative social relationships. . . . It takes at least two to have a right—with the exception of those cases in which one has a right to be treated a certain way by oneself. Rights have sociality built into them."[26] In the exceptional case of the subject possessing the right to be treated a certain way by oneself as Wolterstorff suggests, one can argue healthcare is a right by oneself. "Racial discrimination endures in many areas of American life, including healthcare. A new paper in *Health Affairs,* co-authored by Amitabh Chandra, at Harvard Kennedy School, considers the problem of inadequate or inferior health care of minority patients . . . "[27]

Finally, Wolterstorff grounds rights in the worth of human beings. In the worth of the subject. "Rights represent the interweaving between, on the one hand, ways of being treated that would be a good in our lives, and, on the other hand, the worth that we ourselves have . . . recognition of the worth, the dignity, the estimability of persons and human beings themselves."[28] The negation of the recognition of the worth, which Wolterstorff posits, is a part of the dehumanizing effect or the legacy of slavery, which infantilized black people during slavery and Jim Crow. Writing in *The Cross and the Lynching Tree,* James H. Cone describes this infantilization. "When an adult black male is treated like a child in a patriarchal society—with whites calling him boy, uncle, and

25. King Jr., *A Testament of Hope,* 292–93.
26. Wolterstorff, *Journey Toward Justice,* 44.
27. Gibson, "Healthcare as a civil rights issue," para. 1.
28. Wolterstorff, *Journey Toward Justice,* 49.

nigger—proclaiming oneself a man is a bold and necessary affirmation of black resistance . . . it often had to be camouflaged in
blues songs about sexuality at the juke joint."[29]

Justice and rights, in conversation with theological perspectives from below, represent many varied and diverse voices, often
articulated in the framework of the prism from which they live and
seek justice and rights. Nicholas P. Wolterstorff provides language
to better understand, and to facilitate in-depth discussions around
the focus of justice and rights. It remains, however, that compre-
hending justice and rights, from the perspective of the privileged
and the perspective from below, continues to serve as an impasse
in achieving justice and rights.

29. Cone, *The Cross and The Lynching Tree*, 17.

CHAPTER 4

Reflections upon Nicholas Wolterstorff's "Education and Public Life Together"

I. Introduction

EDUCATION IN THE UNITED States for African Americans, often the descendants of Africans in the diaspora, subordinate only to black religion, has been the singularly most significant medium through which African Americans have pursued freedom and parity in this *"Strange Land."* Titans of the struggle for freedom in the United States, such as Booker T. Washington and W. E. B. Du Bois, have engaged in vigorous debate pertinent to the role education should play in the life of the *Negro*. Carter G. Woodson in his watershed publication *The Mis-Education of the Negro*, lamented the duplication of a European pedagogy ill-suited for Negroes in America and their precarious circumstances. " . . . On the right way to understand the Negro . . . they will serve the Negro much better than those who are trying to find out whether Henry VIII lusted more after Anne Boleyn than after Catherine of Aragon or whether Elizabeth was justly styled as more untruthful than Philip II of Spain."[1]

What is the role of education, for who, to what end(s)? Even in institutions of higher education and theological education, this author has discovered that this question goes largely unresolved. Remnants of the Carter G. Woodson tension are evident, even as descendants of African slaves matriculate at Princeton Seminary, Harvard Divinity, Yale Divinity, and other prestigious institutions of higher learning. This tension manifests in a clash of pedagogical theories of education. In the European pedagogy, abstract theorizing and dialectical reflection are often the accepted gold standard of education. In the African American pedagogy, the ability to concretize and contextualize content has greater utility toward preserving existential existence. This binary is the basis of significant consternation of many students of color, and is exasperated by the dearth of African heritage teachers of color in the academy, and their sensitivity and awareness of this bifurcation.

What then is the goal(s) of education? The answer perhaps lies in one's social location. Aristotle's statement concerning education is very helpful in this moment. "Education is an ornament in prosperity and a refuge in adversity."[2] Life in the United States has been an adversarial space for persons of color. Education that is well informed has been a refuge. Nicholas Wolterstorff's *Education and Public Life Together* is a move that oppressed people find relevant to their experiences in the Diaspora. Wolterstorff illuminates *flourishing, justice, and peace* as the foci of education. Wolterstorff's prescriptions are the negation of *mis-education* for oppressed people. *Educating for shalom,* as Wolterstorff articulates it, has as its goal the fundamental rights of justice for all people. Shalom, as a starting point for education within the African American Community, satisfies Carter G. Woodson's misgivings over the state of affairs relevant to education for the oppressed.

---

1. Woodson, *Mis-Education of the Negro*, 37.
2. Pojman and Vaughn, *Moral Life*, 550.

II. Defining Shalom

Oppressive states often cite the absence of conflict to buttress the argument that the status quo is sufficient. Wolterstorff immediately identifies this for the specious argument that it is. "But shalom goes beyond peace, beyond the absence of hostility. A nation may be at peace and yet be miserable in its poverty. Shalom is not just peace but flourishing, flourishing in all dimensions of our existence . . . "[3]

Wolterstorff emphasizes that shalom is not only peace; however, shalom is an Old Testament declaration of justice. "The Old Testament declarations about justice is the passionate insistence that all the members of the community are entitled to a full and secure place in the life of the community. Hence the clanging repetitive reference to orphans, widows and sojourner."[4]

III. Setting the Context—Identifying the Problem

Injustice does not exist in a vacuum; however, injustice exists in the context of unjust structures of society vis-à-vis legal systems, economic systems, systems of education, as well as any medium designed to marginalize and oppress people. The unsuspecting observer might conclude that the arrangement of the aforementioned systems occur organically, a type of meritocracy formed by ethnicity and race superiority and inferiority, and informed by the survival of the fittest.

Wolterstorff identifies what he refers to as core and periphery within capitalism, which requires exploitation and the negation of flourishing for the majority of people, in order to provide superfluous conspicuous consumption for a minority of people. " . . . The capitalist economy of our world-system has a horizontal structure of core and periphery. . . . Those areas of heaviest capital accumulation constitute the core of the system. . . . A consequence of this

---

3. Wolterstorff, *Educating for Shalom*, 114.

4. Wolterstorff, *Educating for Shalom*, 143.

domination is that the core exploits the periphery . . ."[5] A proper goal of *education and public life together* is to provide students with the tools to deconstruct and elucidate complex systems as a major move toward human flourishing. Oversimplified models, such as "pick yourself up by your bootstraps" and "self-made men and women," along with the so-called "Protestant work ethic," have made their way into the psychology of our culture and education system.

Achieving shalom, which includes flourishing, justice, and peace for Wolterstorff, must provide students with the insightfulness that the foundation for elitism begins early in the educational process. Miguel A. De La Torre chronicles the beginning of elitism in education. "The (class) room is appropriately named, for it is indeed a room of class—a room where students learn the class they belong to and the power and privilege that comes with that class . . . they will have certain opportunities that are denied to those of lower economic classes."[6]

If all people are to experience shalom or flourishing, justice, and peace, then the discourse pertinent to education must concern itself with the ghettoization of education—penthouse education for the desirables of society, and shantytown education for the poor and the marginalized. Unfortunately, in the United States, arguably with the exception of Catholic education, Protestant Christian education has been an opportunity for white flight, for families seeking escape from public schools teeming with students of color. This phenomenon is the redux of the 1896 Plessy v. Ferguson Supreme Court decision, which upheld the separate but equal two-tier education system in America. Education toward achieving shalom must perform an appendectomy on the infected organ of racism resident in public education, and it must be performed by those who are true adherents of the gospel of Jesus Christ.

5. Wolterstorff, *Educating for Shalom*.
6. De La Torre, *Christian Ethics from the Margins*, xi.

IV. Setting the Context—Historical Analysis in the African American Context

The negation of flourishing, justice, and peace has historically had egregious debilitating effects upon the African American community. The Reverend Dr. Martin Luther King Jr. and W. E. B. Du Bois famously chronicled the negation of justice and flourishing in the era of Jim Crow segregation. Dr. King posited that segregation not only established limitations upon the daily interactions of African Americans; however, the malevolent character of segregation debilitated the personality of human beings, a negation of the *imago Dei* central to Christianity and shalom. ". . . Explain to your six-year old daughter why she can't go to the public amusement park . . . and see the depressing clouds of inferiority begin to form in her little mental sky, and see her begin to distort her little personality . . ."[7]

The *seed*, the very *contaminant* or *germ* borrowing from Schleiermacher, in this instance pertaining to segregation, or the negation of justice, has its power in the replicability of resentment transplanted into the hearts and minds of its victims. The result is a vicious cycle of hatred, retribution, and what contemporary social scientists refer to as *internalized racist oppression*, or hatred of the self as a result of the constant attack on the psychology of black personality. W. E. B. Du Bois identified this phenomenon in what he famously referred to as *double consciousness*. " . . . Du Bois used 'double consciousness' to refer to at least three different issues—including first the real power of white stereotypes in black life and thought and second the double consciousness created by the practical racism that excluded every black American from the mainstream of the society . . ."[8]

There has been no shortage of postulations for the hegemony of white people over black people in the United States; the so-called *curse of Ham* as a pseudo-theology is one explanation, followed by the telling of revisionist history presenting slavery as an innocuous

7. King Jr., *A Testament of Hope*, 292–93.
8. Du Bois, *Souls of Black Folk*, 238.

and benevolent haven for Africans in America. Reinhold Niebuhr theorizes that the negation of flourishing is endemic to the human condition. " . . . That fullness of life which each man seeks. However much human ingenuity may increase the treasures . . . they can never be sufficient to satisfy all human wants; for man, unlike other creatures, is gifted and cursed with an imagination which extends his appetites beyond the requirements of subsistence."[9] Africans in America have been instrumentalized historically to serve the purpose of satisfying the excessive appetites of white America.

V. Moves Toward Resolution: Wolterstorff / Rawls / Rousseau

Perhaps the condition of Sisyphus in *Homer's Odyssey* best describes the work of educating for shalom in the world. The work of seeking human flourishing, justice, and peace is a never-ending intentional struggle to achieve parity for an often despised people.

It is imperative that those educating for shalom have a profound, comprehensive understanding of the complexities of systems operative which negate human flourishing. Many of these dehumanizing systems are so interwoven into the culture and mores of society, that only the most discriminating pedagogical methods are able to elucidate the mechanisms imperative for their insidious telos. Those educating for shalom must dispense with Pollyannaish Christian identity inextricably tied to nationalism, patriotism, and culture. Wolterstorff reiterates the importance of serious reflection upon the goal of educating for shalom. "My aim is to lead us in reflecting together on how students can be led into rejecting all those actualities of our society, and all those possibilities it pursues, which oppress people and deprive them of their rights, which violate justice."[10]

Educating for shalom requires empathetic vicarious imagination. John Rawls demonstrates this empathetic vicarious

---

9. Niebuhr, *Moral Man*, 1.

10. Wolterstorff, *Educating for Shalom*, 136.

imagination in his *veil of ignorance.* "First of all, no one knows his place in society, his class position or social status; nor does he know his fortune in the distribution of natural assets and abilities, his intelligence and strength, and the like. Nor, again . . . the particulars of his rational plan of life . . . "[11] Wolterstorff amplifies the intent of Rawls and the *veil of ignorance,* in his discussion of the Good Samaritan in *Justice in Love.* "I take Jesus to be enjoining us to be alert to the obligations placed upon us by the needs of whomever we happen on, and to pay no attention to the fact, if it be a fact, that the needy person belongs to a group that is a disdained or disdaining out-group . . . "[12]

The social contract philosopher Jean-Jacques Rousseau captures the essence of shalom in *Discourse on the Origin of Inequality.* "The first man who, having fenced in a piece of land, said 'This is mine,' . . . From how many crimes, wars, and murders . . . might not any one have saved mankind, by filling up the ditch, and crying . . . you are undone if you once forget that the fruits of the earth belong to us all, and the earth itself to nobody."[13]

The goal of *education and public life together* is, through imagination informed by justice, to respect the rights of all humanity to flourish and realize the potential of his or her personhood, while sharing the resources of our world equitably to the glory of God.

11. Rawls, *A Theory of Justice,* 118.
12. Wolterstorff, *Acting Liturgically,* 250.
13. Rousseau, *Discourse on Inequality,* 23.

CHAPTER 5

A Century
of African American Excellence

The Genius of Unheralded Leaders
of African American Religious Experience

The *black pulpit*, historically has been the locus of black resistance and prophetic voice in America speaking from the margins. For nearly a century, the black Preacher integrated religion, politics, and the academy in *Speaking Truth to Power*. This period marks the magnum opus of black religious prophetic voice emanating from the black church.

Arguably, Dietrich Bonhoeffer captured best the sentiment that those who are marginalized in society, those who are disenfranchised, those who are powerless, are best situated to serve as the moral conscience of a community. Writing in *The View from Below*, Bonhoeffer states this with marked clarity. "It remains an experience of incomparable value that we have for once learned to see the great events of world history from below, from the perspective of the outcasts . . . in short from the perspective of the suffering . . . that we come to see . . . clearer, freer, more incorruptible."[1]

1. Bonhoeffer, *The Bonhoeffer Reader*, 775.

The lived experience in the United States has been a type of *view from below* for Africans in the Diaspora in America. Black religious leaders have demonstrated extraordinary theological imagination in order to survive enslavement, Jim Crow apartheid, and lynching as a systematic method of genocide. The black preacher wielded the power and influence of the pulpit, the academy, and the political apparatus, to stoke the dreams of the black community through inspired theological imagination. This is often what makes black preaching, the black pulpit, and the black preacher unique in the context of the religious experience in America. James H. Cone, writing in *The Cross and the Lynching Tree*, makes the following observation. "People without imagination really have no right to write about ultimate things, Reinhold Niebuhr was correct to observe. No one can claim that black preachers' sermonic orations lacked rhetorical imagination."[2]

The black preacher, black theologian, and black academic synthesized into one discipline what the white church understood as a binary; the pulpit was the domain of the preacher, the academy was the domain of the scholar, and the body politic was given expression through the work of the politician. In black America, no such luxury existed for black people. Perhaps this is a reality inherited by black people from African traditional religion, which understands no arbitrary lines of demarcation, separating religious experience from the all-encompassing lived experience. J. Omosade Awolalu writing in *Yoruba Beliefs and Sacrificial Rites* clarifies this phenomenon. "In spite of the varied forms and systems, religious consciousness permeates every portion of African life; secularity has no reality in the African existence . . . contemporary African scholars believe that generally all people and groups of Africa believe in a supreme, self-existent deity."[3] Black people in America instinctively understood that their personality, and hence their worth as human beings, derived from their creator as expressed in the biblical text and understood through

---

2. Cone, *The Cross and The Lynching Tree*, 94.

3. Grant, "Ancient African Religion," para. 22.

the black hermeneutic. The black preacher gave expression to this imagination.

Given a different reality there may have been no necessity to synthesize the church, academy, and political life. The genius of the black preacher was his (male-dominated misogyny perhaps) ability to deconstruct the hegemonic systems of oppression, and to lay bare the racist structural underpinnings of society. The racism, and racist ideologies, informing the society were more often than not perpetuated through the structures of the white church and Eurocentric pedagogy of academia. The black preacher helped to elucidate these systems and interpret them to the larger society.

Miguel A. De La Torre, writing in *Doing Christian Ethics from the Margins*, informs how the dominant culture instrumentalizes morality, ethics, and religion to perpetuate a society that preserves the status quo. "As long as the religious leaders and scholars of the dominant culture continue to construct ethical perspectives from within their cultural space of wealth and power, the marginalized will need an alternative format by which to deliberate and, more importantly, do ethics."[4] The black preacher and the black pulpit provided that alternative format through their prophetic imaginative voice and activism. Black churches around the United States were transformed into *war rooms* for strategizing and staging the resistance. "Through critical social analysis, it is possible to uncover the connection existing between the prevailing ideologies that support the present power arrangement, with the political, economic, and cultural components of the mechanisms of oppression that protect their power and wealth."[5] Often, sermons originating in the black pulpit uncovered the connection referenced.

Despite the fact that Christianity in America was often weaponized to destroy the fabric of black life, and to maintain black people as second class citizens, black religion proved to be resilient in the face of this dialectic. Howard Thurman in *Jesus And The Disinherited* mused pensively concerning the seeming inability of Christianity to serve as a corrective to this glaring dialectic. "

4. De La Torre, *Christian Ethics from the Margins*, 5.

5. De La Torre, *Christian Ethics from the Margins*, 5.

. . . Christianity seems impotent to deal radically, and therefore effectively, with the issues of discrimination and injustice on the basis of race, religion and national origin? Is this impotency due to a betrayal of the genius of the religion, or is it due to a basic weakness in the religion itself?"[6]

Cone responds to the crisis of faith inherent in the black religious experience. Making use of W. E. B. Du Bois, Cone answers Howard Thurman. "Somewhat like his use of the concept of double consciousness to explain the African American search for identity, Du Bois used the paradox of faith and doubt together to explain the meaning of the black religious experience."[7] In a move that embraces the reality of doubt intermingling with faith, it affirms the resilience of black religion, in the face of powers which seek to threaten the existential reality of black life. "One cannot correctly understand the black religious experience without an affirmation of deep faith informed by profound doubt. Suffering naturally gives rise to doubt."[8]

Black religious leaders were astute enough to discern the deception of oppressive tactics. White clergy, beginning in slavery and thereafter, often countered the civil rights ideas of the Reverend Dr. Martin Luther King Jr. by appealing to black people to be good slaves, and then in the twentieth century to be good law abiding citizens. To adhere to the religious tenets of Rom 13 and respect the governing bodies both local and federal. Dietrich Bonhoeffer describes this type of deception. Clifford Green and Michael DeJonge observe in *The Bonhoeffer Reader* what Bonhoeffer refers to as *Satan's truth*. "There is a such thing as Satan's truth. Its nature is to deny everything real under the guise of the truth. It feeds on hatred against the real, against the world created and loved by God. . . . Satan's truth judges what is created out of envy and hatred."[9]

---

6. Thurman, *Jesus and the Disinherited*, 7.

7. Cone, *The Cross and the Lynching Tree*, 106.

8. Cone, *The Cross and the Lynching Tree*, 106.

9. Bonhoeffer, *The Bonhoeffer Reader*, 754.

Those white clergy who value law and order, as well as property, do so at the expense of the black community. Their insistence upon adherence to the letter of the law, as opposed to the intent of the law to facilitate human flourishing, is a legalistic ethical insistence. It is a Satan's truth. De La Torre, in a type of transvaluation, explains how his mother, an immigrant with no work experience neither the ability to speak English, negotiated laws in place that would potentially shut her out of the workplace. "If she demonstrated the virtue of honesty . . . she would never have been hired. Yet, the moral reasoning she employed enabled her to surmount societal structures fundamentally averse to her very existence. Which is more ethical . . . doing what needs to be done to get the job, or letting the sins of others force us to live on the street?"[10]

The black preacher was able to transvalue Christianity and principle to empower people of color. This is the genius of black religion.

Reverend Dr. Mordecai Wyatt Johnson represents the genius of the black church and the historically black college and university. Mordecai Johnson was born in Tennessee in the year 1890. Johnson was the son of Wyatt and Carolyn Johnson, who had been born into slavery. Most accounts of Mordecai Johnson's birth indicate that he was the legitimate son of Wyatt, who was a former slave. This claim presents a difficulty. It is a difficulty that is very familiar to those who are a part of the African American community. One of the striking physical characteristics of Mordecai Johnson is that one would not necessarily know that he was an African American man. Mordecai Johnson by any rational assessment has the appearance in hue and physical features of European descent. This is not uncommon in African American communities; however, it has been and continues to be a point of contention. It is difficult to fathom the idea, or to reconcile the claim, that Mordecai Johnson is the progeny of Wyatt and Carolyn Johnson, and not the offspring of a forced relationship between a former slave owner and Carolyn. This is conjecture. It is significant nonetheless, due

10. De La Torre, *Christian Ethics from the Margins*, 22.

to the fact that fairer skinned African Americans historically were afforded opportunities denied darker skinned African Americans.

Lawrence Otis Graham, a Princeton University alumnus, writing in *Our Kind of People: Inside America's Black Upper Class*, makes the following observation. "It was a color thing and a class thing. And for generations of black people, color and class have been inexorably tied together. Since I was born and raised around people with a focus on many of these characteristics . . . that I was later to decide . . . to have my nose surgically altered."[11] Such a conscientious decision would have less to do with aesthetics, and more to do with acceptance within the circles of the black bourgeoisie. Graham continues, " . . . So that I could further buy into the aesthetic biases that many among the black elite hold so dear."[12] Historically, it has been an unmistakably salient feature of some of the preferred leadership, by both white and black America, that African American institutions vis-à-vis the church and academy, be presided over by fair skinned black men. W. E. B. Du Bois, Mordecai Johnson, Adam Clayton Powell Jr., to name only a few, are each capable of *passing*. In an article titled *A Chosen Exile: Black People Passing In White America*, Karen Grigsby Bates makes the following observation. "Loss of self. Loss of family. Loss of community. Loss of the ability to answer honestly the question black people have been asking each other since before Emancipation: Who are your people?"[13]

The trauma of slavery and Jim Crow created a caste system within black America, which extends into one's religious experience as well. Who are your people, and what church do you belong to, were queries associated with what opportunities will be afforded one. "They already knew about the obsession our group had with Episcopal churches, good hair, light complexions, the AKAs, and Martha's Vineyard."[14] Unbeknownst to most, W. E. B. Du Bois' *double consciousness* does not only originate from outside of black

11. Graham, *Our Kind of People*, 4.

12. Graham, *Our Kind of People*, 4.

13. "'A Chosen Exile,'" para. 12.

14. Graham, *Our Kind of People*, xvii.

America, however, but from within the black community as well. "
. . . A two-ness of being an American, a Negro; two warring ideals
in one dark body, whose dogged strength alone keeps it from being torn asunder."[15]

Despite the binary created by the color issue in America,
Mordecai Johnson set out to transform black America. Johnson
came to the presidency of Howard University in the year 1926,
during the time in which one of his most accomplished faculty,
and there were many, Alain LeRoy Locke, coined the phrase *new
Negro*. Henry Louis Gates, writing in an article titled "The New
Negro and the Black Image: From Booker T. Washington to Alain
Locke," makes the following observation. "The New Negro . . .
have risen since the war, with education, refinement, and money.
In marked contrast with their enslaved or disenfranchised ances-
tors, these New Negroes demanded that their rights as citizens
be vouchsafed by law. Significantly, these New Negroes were to
be recognized by their education . . . "[16] Mordecai Johnson, the
institution's inaugural black president, laid the foundation for its
unofficial name of *the black mecca* and the so-called new Negro.
Johnson would lead Howard University for thirty-four years. During his tenure some of the greatest intellectuals served as faculty
members, and Howard University became a significant influence
pertinent to shaping black culture and intellectual life.

During Johnson's tenure at Howard University, he continued
to preach in pulpits around America, and became recognized as
one of the great orators of black preaching, a skill he perfected as
the pastor of First Baptist Church in West Virginia from 1917 to
1926.

Illustrative of the indispensable relationship between black
religion and black intellectualism is the famous Andrew Rankin
Memorial Chapel at Howard University. "Over the decades, some
of the most renowned and distinguished orators of the world have
spoken in the Chapel . . . It was here that Dr. Mordecai Wyatt Johnson, the first African American president of Howard University,

15. Du Bois, *Souls of Black Folk*, 236.

16. Gates Jr., "The New Negro," para. 3.

thundered his sermons against McCarthyism, racism, ignorance and squalor."[17] Historically, in black America, religion and academia complement one another. There is no sense of tension or schism between the two as institutions. One could walk into a classroom at Howard University and hear renowned scientist Dr. Charles Drew discuss blood transfusions, and then walk across campus to Rankin Memorial Chapel and hear black preaching. "This beautiful and historic building has been graced by . . . the most distinguished American preachers such as Vernon Johns, Martin Luther King Jr., Samuel Proctor, Gardner Taylor, William Holmes Borders, Reinhold Niebuhr, and Howard Thurman."[18]

The black church, coterminous with the historically black college and university, served as the architects of resistance and protest in America. It also provided a domain for black dignity and flourishing away from the slights and prejudices of white America.

Benjamin Elijah Mays served as one of those architects alongside of Mordecai Johnson in shaping the black religious landscape. Mays has often been cited as being the intellectual force behind the civil rights movement strategic decisions. Martin Luther King Jr. referred to Mays as his spiritual mentor. Like Mordecai Johnson, Benjamin E. Mays was both an ordained Baptist minister and the leader of the prestigious Morehouse College in Atlanta, Georgia. Mays was appointed as the sixth president in 1940, and his tenure lasted until 1967, during which time he presided over significant growth both in terms of financial support, as well as prominence. Prior to his appointment as president of Morehouse College, Mays served as the Dean of the School of Religion at Howard University.

What is less appreciated and understood is the role the black pulpit and black minister assumed in shaping the black college and university. The presidents of the schools were ministers. By extension then, the black pulpit helped to inform both the trajectory of black higher education, as well as the pedagogy of black higher education. Many of the historically black colleges and universities were founded as Bible institutions. An example of this is Albany

17. Howard University, "Andrew Rankin Memorial Chapel," para. 2.
18. Howard University, "Andrew Rankin Memorial Chapel," para. 3.

State University in Albany, Georgia, founded in 1903 as the Albany Bible and Manual Training Institute, by Joseph Winthrop Holley who himself aspired to be a minister, of which this author is an alumnus.

One of the final acts for the Reverend Dr. Martin Luther King Jr. was the eulogy given by Benjamin E. Mays, as a fitting exclamation upon the intertwined nature of the pulpit and the academy. Where the pulpit ends and the academy begins in black religion is indistinguishable. The relationship between the two men was extensive and culminated only in death. Mays stated memorably, "No! He was not ahead of his time. No man is ahead of his time. Every man is within his star, each in his time."[19]

The black pulpit has been the locus of black resistance and the prophetic voice in America speaking from the margins. The greatest period in black religion, the magnum opus of the black church, could serve as the blueprint to inform present and future generations of black leadership, in resisting oppression and racism in America. Black Lives Matter and other movements would do well to be instructed by their predecessors and their voices emanating from black religion.

19. Mays, "Benjamin Mays, Class of 1920," para. 20.

CHAPTER 6

Reflection on Lynching in Jim Crow America

In Conversation with James Cone and Jürgen Moltmann

I. Introduction

HISTORICALLY, SUFFERING OR THE retelling of people's suffering throughout history has been an aspect of the human narrative through ethnography, didactic literature, religious scholarship, anthropology, and other forms of documentation. Whether the Jewish Holocaust, ethnic cleansing in Kosovo, genocide in Rwanda, or lynching in the Jim Crow South, it is imperative that the victims of these atrocities have their stories not only told, but however, reevaluated and reenvisioned with critical tools and thoughtful imagination.

Here, the critical tool and thoughtful imagination is leveraged through the works of James Cone, *The Cross and the Lynching Tree* in conversation with Jürgen Moltmann in *The Crucified God*. More directly, can both African Americans and their descendants, who suffered ineffable heinous atrocities perpetrated upon them during the Jim Crow era through lynching and terrorism, find meaning and thereby consolation through the 'theological reopening' of these cases, as though a cold case of sorts in theological parlance? As in a cold case new evidence is introduced and new conclusions drawn. With the aid of Cone and Moltmann through transvaluation, the theological perspective of the cross will illuminate the hope of the victims of Jim Crow terrorism.

II. Setting the Context

The biblical text found in Rev 7 describes a multitude of people who are depicted as having come through great suffering and tribulation. What is uncertain is exactly who this demographic is. What is clear is that they are the collective suffering of people from around the world. Are they the "Crucified People"? Are they the genocide victims of Rwanda? Is this great multitude the victims of lynching in the Jim Crow South? One difficulty is that theologians who do theology from the dominant culture, or what is referred to as from the top as opposed to from the bottom, or from the margins, are inclined to examine this question strictly from an exegetical lens.

Reenvisioning this biblical text from an oppressed hermeneutic creates a space to consider the suffering people of Rev 7 as the genocide victims of Rwanda, the ethnic cleansing victims of Kosovo, or other historically victimized people such as the Jewish people of the Holocaust. In *The Cross And The Lynching Tree*, James Cone makes use of the phenomenon of imagination in order to extrapolate from one historical event to another, at times spanning centuries. Cone is very critical of those who are unable to employ imagination to make use of both historical symbols and events, to inform contemporary crises and human dilemmas of various sorts. In the case of Cone, he is critical of theologians who are unable, or unwilling, to extrapolate from the events surrounding the crucifixion of Jesus, to the victims of the lynching tree during the era of systematic lynching in the Jim Crow South. "The crucifixion of Jesus by the Romans in Jerusalem and the lynching of blacks by whites in the United States are so amazingly similar that one wonders what blocks the American Christian imagination from seeing the connection."[1] Imagination, or lack of imagination, is a metanarrative throughout Cone's writing.

It is not theologically unsound, nor academically unsuitable, to invoke the tool of imagination or a reenvisioned hermeneutic to give eschatological hope to the "Lynched People," through reenvisioning them as part of the redeemed people in Rev 7. "People without imagination really have no right to write about ultimate things, Reinhold Niebuhr was correct to observe."[2]

Hope is a major theological precept of Moltmann's theology. In *Theology of Hope* Moltmann writes, "Totally without hope one cannot live. To live without hope is to cease to live. Hell is hopelessness. It is not accident that above the entrance to Dante's hell is the inscription: Leave behind all hope, you who enter here."[3] For many of the Lynched People, there was no hope in the Jim Crow South. Christ recrucified recalls for some author Nikos Kazantzakis, James Cone, and other theologians perhaps. When people are too dismissive of the reenvisioning of the Lynched People through imagination, as part of the Rev 7 community, it recrucifies the Lynched People through the removal of hope, and empowers the imaginers of evil through lynching and crucifixion and gives them the final say. Hope is the Yes to the lynchers' No.

God's identification with the Lynched People of Mississippi is the negation of the power of the lynchers. As Moltmann writes in *The Crucified God* concerning God in Auschwitz, "Then God will turn his sorrow into eternal joy . . . the overcoming of the history of man's sorrow and the fulfillment of his history of hope. God in Auschwitz and Auschwitz in the crucified God . . . "[4] Another rendering of Moltmann might be, God in Mississippi and Mississippi in the crucified God.

1. Cone, *The Cross and the Lynching Tree*, 31.
2. Cone, *The Cross and the Lynching Tree*, 94.
3. Moltmann, *Theology of Hope*, 32.
4. Moltmann, *The Crucified God*, 417.

"And so my friends, they did not die in vain, (Yeah) God still has a way of wringing good out of evil. (Oh yes) And history has proven over and over again that unmerited suffering is redemptive."[5] These are the words of The Reverend Dr. Martin Luther King Jr. at the eulogy for the little school-aged girls killed on September 15, 1963, at 16th Street Baptist Church in Birmingham, Alabama. It is beyond the scope of this research to argue the merits of salvific suffering. The topic nonetheless deserves a cursory reflection in the context of the Lynched People and their suffering.

Many renowned womanist theologians, feminist theologians, as well as a new wave of millennial theologians argue against the idea of suffering as salvific or having any redemptive qualities. The logic is that somehow the idea of salvific suffering glorifies suffering, a type of sadistic masochism. This fails to take into consideration the dialectic of the cross. The dialectic of the cross is the transvaluation of defeat, and the whole of the Beatitudes of Jesus rendered in the Sermon on the Mount. Each tenet of the Beatitudes is a transvaluation of human understanding, and everything that is counterintuitive to what society deems as strong. One can make the argument that salvific suffering is consistent with the transvaluation of human values, and consistent with the logic of the Beatitudes. Reinhold Niebuhr characterized the whole of Christianity in the context of transvaluation. "Or as Niebuhr put it, The Christian faith is centered in one who was born in a manger and who dies upon the cross. This is really the source of the Christian transvaluation of all values."[6]

Mark Twain, in a famous essay written in 1901, best captured the climate in America in his titled essay, "The United States of Lyncherdom." "MT wrote this essay in the summer of 1901, in reaction to a newspaper account of the Missouri lynching he mentions at the start. . . . I shouldn't have even half a friend left down there [in the South], after it issued from the press."[7]

5. King Jr., *A Testament of Hope*, 222.

6. Cone, *The Cross and the Lynching Tree*, 36.

7. Twain, "United States of Lyncherdom," para. 1.

The history of the Lynched People in the United States, as well as the "Crucified People" of the world, is to recall some of the most horrific periods not only in American history; however, it is to recall some of the most hideous crimes against humanity in human world history. It is a cautionary tale to recall Moltmann's admonition that Christ died not only for the victims of crimes against humanity, but also the perpetrators of the lynchings, the Adolf Eichmann's of the world who orchestrated the logistics of the Holocaust concentration camps, the Hutu who engaged in the genocide of the Tutsi of Rwanda, lest the most human of responses to hate becomes one's obsession. "The one will triumph who first died for the victims then also for the executioners, and in so doing revealed a new righteousness which breaks through vicious circles of hate and vengeance and which from the lost victims and executioners creates a new mankind with a new humanity."[8] It is the search for, and the incessant need to recall, this 'new righteousness' that informs the recounting of the stories of the Lynched People in the United States, lest one succumb to the siren call of hatred informed by years of victimization.

III. Telling the Story

In the summer of 1955, Chicago native Emmett Till would unwittingly become a central figure in the Civil Rights movement in the United States. What would transpire in August of that year would shock the conscience of the country, and would place front and center the brutal and inhumane culture of Jim Crow lynching. Till, from the North and accustomed to the culture and mores of northern culture, allegedly transgressed one of the taboo rites of southern culture—the intermingling of the races between gender lines. Paradoxically, this southern rite of forbidden miscegenation was forced upon African American women as part of the rights of white men during the era of slavery; as well, white men raped

8. Moltmann, *The Crucified God*, 178.

African American girls and women with impunity during the Jim Crow era.

In the case of Till, he is alleged to have whistled at a young white woman while visiting a country store. "In August 1955, 14 year-old Chicago resident Emmett Till . . . accompanied Till's great-uncle Mose Wright back to Wright's home in Mississippi. . . . There, Till was briefly alone in Bryant's Grocery with . . . white store clerk Carolyn Bryant. . . . Till apparently whistled at her—a dangerous breach of Mississippi racial etiquette."[9] In retribution of this transgression, Till was abducted from the home of his relatives, tortured by beating, and genital castration, by some accounts while he was still alive, and finally thrown into the Tallahatchie River in Mississippi. The castration of lynching victims was customary, and served as a reminder that white men would protect the virtuousness of white women. Following a very brief kangaroo court in Mississippi, an all white jury engaged in jury nullification finding the accused not guilty.

It is believed by many in the African American community, this writer not excluded, that the jury nullification years later in the case of Orenthal James Simpson, otherwise known as O. J. Simpson, in the killing of Nicole Brown and Ron Goldman, is a classic case of the long memories of African Americans enduring the jury nullifications of lynching victims of the Jim Crow South. African Americans were erudite enough, though without formal education or legal training, to interpret within the American legal system there existed a corruption or miscarriage of justice. It is what Dietrich Bonhoeffer would refer to as "Satan's Truth" in his text, "What Does it Mean to Tell the Truth?"[10] The scales of justice did not reflect justice for the Lynched People of the South, only white people. For African Americans there was no semblance of truth or justice in the law, only an insidious form of judicial lynching. "There is such a thing as Satan's truth. Its nature is to deny everything real under the guise of truth. It feeds on hatred against

9. Wagner, "America's Civil Rights Revolution," 188.
10. In Bonhoeffer, *The Bonhoeffer Reader*.

the real, against the world created and loved by God."[11] For African Americans, "Satan's Truth" informed the legal system under Jim Crow and afforded no justice.

It is remarkable that African Americans, the descendants of slaves, embrace Christianity at all. The imagination that is necessary to parse biblical text and find within it a theology that speaks to their context is a testimony of their will to survive in a hostile land. The loss of faith is perhaps the greatest tragedy suffered by victims of terrorism. One account of a freed African American speaks to the tension between faith and suffering, as they attempted to reconcile the promises of their faith and the incongruence of the actions of white people, in particular white Christians who professed faith in the same God and Jesus Christ, and yet held them in bondage and lynching in the South. " . . . To know why the good Lord should so long afflict my people, and keep them in bondage—to be abused, and trampled down . . . with no ray of light in the future. Some of my folks said there wasn't any God, for if there was he wouldn't let white folks do as they do for so many years."[12] Elie Wiesel captured this tension writing in *Night* as a concentration camp detainee recounts the occasion of his loss of faith. "Never shall I forget that night, the first night in camp. . . . Never shall I forget those moments which murdered my God and my soul and turned my dreams to dust . . . even if I am condemned to live as long as God Himself."[13]

The 1963 bombing of the 16th Street Baptist Church in Birmingham, Alabama, was a seminal moment in not only the Civil Rights Movement but in America as well. Some would place this event as one of the markers indicating the moment the United States lost its soul. "On Sunday, 15th September, 1963, a white man was seen getting out of a white and turquoise Chevrolet car and placing a box under the steps of the Sixteenth Street Baptist Church . . . the bomb exploded killing Denise McNair . . . Addie Mae Collins

---

11. Bonhoeffer, *The Bonhoeffer Reader*, 752.

12. Cone, *The Cross and the Lynching Tree*, 123.

13. Wiesel, *Night*, 32.

... Carole Robertson ... Cynthia Wesley."[14] The bombing shocked the conscience of the American people, both black and white. It was one of the most heinous crimes perpetrated against African American people, even when lynching is taken into account.

The act was so unthinkable that it prompted a white attorney in Birmingham, Charles Morgan, to find the moral courage, and to speak these immortal words. "Four little girls were killed in Birmingham yesterday. . . . Who did it? Who threw that bomb? . . . We all did it. Every last one of us is condemned. . . . We all did it."[15]

The Reverend Dr. Martin Luther King Jr., in his eulogy for Addie Mae Collings, Cynthia Wesley, Carole Robertson, and Carol Denise McNair, captured the dialectic of the beauty of these children, their innocence, in juxtaposition with the ugliness and savagery of the bombing. Dr. King closed the eulogy with these beautiful words. "Shakespeare had Horatio utter some beautiful words over the dead body of Hamlet. I paraphrase these words today as I stand over the last remains of these lovely girls. Goodnight sweet princesses; may the flight of angels take thee to thy eternal rest."[16]

IV. Responses to *The Crucified God* and *The Cross and the Lynching Tree*

"When God becomes man in Jesus of Nazareth, he not only enters into the finitude of man, but in his death on the cross also enters into the situation of man's godforsakenness. In Jesus he does not die the natural death of a finite being, but the violent death of the criminal on the cross . . . "[17] Moltmann theologically places the crucified God in the midst of the Lynched People, not as one that rescues them from their predicament, and therefore answers the historic theodicy question of why God allowed the enslavement

14. Lezama, *Civil Rights Pioneers*, 51.

15. Cohen, "Speech That Shocked Birmingham," para. 3.

16. King Jr., *A Testament of Hope*, 223.

17. Moltmann, *The Crucified God*, 276.

and suffering of the Lynched People; however, in Moltmann's statement, God is in solidarity with the suffering people as he also enters into the state of godforsakenness through the man Jesus of Nazareth.

The Lynched People are not able to "have this cup pass from them," but rather drink from the same cup of Jesus and all of the suffering people of history. Moltmann places suffering and love as an inextricable theological principle of God. "Were God incapable of suffering in any respect . . . then he would also be incapable of love. If love is the acceptance of the other without regard to one's own wellbeing, then it contains within itself the possibility of sharing in suffering and freedom to suffer . . ."[18]

Suffering therefore illuminates the love God has for the Lynched People, the "Crucified People," the people of the Jewish Holocaust, all as sharing the godforsakenness in their lynchings and suffering. Moltmann makes use of transvaluation pertinent to suffering, as perceived by the powerful people of history, by those who view suffering as weakness, the Friedrich Wilhelm Nietzsche's of the world. A type of slave morality according to Nietzsche. " . . . Those qualities which serve to alleviate the existence of sufferers . . . it is here that sympathy, the kind, helping hand, the warm heart, patience, diligence, humility, and friendliness attain to honor . . . Slave-morality . . . "[19] In the transvaluation of the crucified God, the Lynched People find meaning, dignity, and are empowered with the negation of death as the final humility in a dystopic life of suffering and meaninglessness.

The Lynched People reclaimed the meaning of the cross from a theology of misappropriation, by the oppressors who held them in bondage and servitude. Although Christianity, and its primary symbol being that of the cross, was a place of solace in desperate circumstances, it nonetheless was a symbol of contradictions. "How could Jesus' death in Jerusalem save blacks from mob violence nearly two thousand years later in America? What did salvation mean for African Americans who had to 'walk through

18. Moltmann, *The Crucified God*, 230.
19. Nietzsche, "Slave and Master Morality," 112.

the valley of the shadow of death,' of those forced to swing from a lynching tree?"[20]

Black religion embraces the cross and the narrative of Jesus as savior, both theologically and culturally. Unlike any other culture, black religion permeates all spheres of black life. In popular culture the figure of Jesus moves seamlessly between black music, theatre, and other forms of genre, perhaps borrowing from the ATR (African traditional religion) experience, which makes no delineation between the sacred and the secular. This is clearly exemplified in popular artists such as Kanye West in his award-winning song "Jesus Walks," or Snoop Dogg's song "Blessing Me Again."

But this does not suggest that African Americans have not historically, and do not now, struggle with the reconciliation of the cross and black life and suffering. African Americans are well aware of the shared relationship of Christianity with the white oppressors of history. The religion that helped African Americans to survive is the religion that was instrumental in their near genocide. "White ministers sometimes served as mob leaders, blessing lynchings, or citing the stories of Ham and Cain to justify white supremacy as a divine right."[21] The cross is the symbol used by the white terrorist Ku Klux Klan organization and often present at lynchings. "While the cross symbolized God's supreme love for human life, the lynching tree was the most terrifying symbol of hate in America. King held these symbols together in a Hegelian dialectic, a contradiction of thesis and antithesis, yielding to a creative synthesis."[22]

V. Moltmann and Cone: Conclusion

Traditional Western theology as written by proponents representative of the dominant culture, or those in power, is inadequate to tell the story of the Lynched People in a way that is liberating and

---

20. Cone, *The Cross and the Lynching Tree*, 76.

21. Cone, *The Cross and the Lynching Tree*, 76.

22. Cone, *The Cross and the Lynching Tree*, 70.

meaningful for African Americans and their descendants. Through James H. Cone and Jürgen Moltmann, a theology is developed that attempts to make sense of the nonsensical experience of African Americans in the Jim Crow South. This theology struggles to answer some of the most perplexing questions the Lynched People and their descendants must reconcile on a regular basis. "Black suffering needs radical and creative voices . . . who can tell brutal and beautiful stories of how oppressed black people survived with a measure of dignity. . . . Why are we here? And what must we do to achieve our full humanity in a world that denies it?"[23] Moltmann and Cone in *The Crucified God* and *The Cross And The Lynching Tree* take strides to begin this theologically difficult conversation.

23. Cone, *The Cross and the Lynching Tree*, 95.

CHAPTER 7

Early European Work House and Contemporary Penitentiary in the United States

I. Introduction

SOCIETIES FROM EIGHTEENTH- AND nineteenth-century Europe, to nineteenth- throughout twenty-first-century United States, have pursued means through which to manage its population of both indigent and undesirable classes of people. These means manifested in the creation of the work houses of nineteenth-century Europe, informed by the Poor Law Amendment Act of 1834, as well as the prison industrial complex in the United States informed by the Convict Lease System of 1846, and the Three Strikes Law of 1994, and giving rise to the prison industrial complex to include for-profit privatization of jails and prisons in the twentieth century. The work house of Europe and the prison industrial complex of the United States are, and have been historically, used as institutions for social control of the poor and marginalized of their respective societies.

The work houses of Europe and the jails and prisons of the United States are at times indistinguishable. The architecture of both structures are often configured in almost identical manner with spiral corridors extending out from a main housing unit. The deplorable living conditions found in the work houses of Europe, and American jails and prisons are yet another point of similarity. The proximity of the Poor Law Amendment Act of 1834 and the work houses in Europe, as well as the Convict Lease System of 1846 in the United States, span a very brief time frame of twelve years. Although it is unproven that the Convict Lease System was informed by the work houses of Europe, both enterprises served as *de facto* institutions of confinement and control over marginalized populations.

II. Context / Conditions / History Leading to Creation of Work House

With the progress of mechanization or what is known as manufacturing, the advances gained during the early period in European history are undeniable. Manufacturing witnessed the production of goods at a rate of production that was heretofore unprecedented. Through manufacturing, machines enabled the production of goods such as cotton and wool to be produced exponentially faster and more economically than manual laborers. William Radcliffe, writing in *Spinning and Weaving* makes the following observation. "If then by the use of Machines, the Manufacture of cotton . . . has met with such amazing success, may not greater advantages be reasonably expected from cultivating to the utmost the Manufacture of woollen."[1]

The unbridled optimism expressed by the beneficiaries of this burgeoning industry of manufacturing is only matched by the despair of the artisans of the old handcrafted modes of production. As machinery replaced the need for woollen spinning for instance, the impact was disproportionally felt by female workers. Radcliffe

1. Radcliffe, *Origin of the New System*, 139.

highlights this misfortune. "The Combers being men and boys may possibly turn to some other work, but it is not so much with the wife and daughters of the day-laborers . . . who deprived of Woollen Spinning have no other employment."[2]

The impact of manufacturing was decried as having other unexpected, yet insidious consequences, well beyond the loss of wages. Manufacturing began to have a negative cumulative effect upon the economic and social milieu of individuals and families dependent upon an agrarian way of life. Radcliffe observes, "I am better able to relate particularly how the change from the old system of hand-labor to the new one of machinery operated in raising the price of land in the subdivision I am speaking of."[3] The price of progress, or the transition from the so-called old system to the new reality of manufacturing, is the inevitability of the marginally poor, or the so-called respectably poor, falling into the ranks of the poor who are unable to sustain a living wage sufficient to prevent them from descending into poverty. Radcliffe writes, "One of the formidable consequences of this change now began to make its appearance, the poor's rate, which previous to this change had only been known in a comparatively nominal way . . . "[4]

Historically, Europe attempted to address the needs of the poor through its extensive regulation of alms for the poor—how the poor were categorized and how the distribution of alms would be allocated. The able-bodied poor were distinguished from the poor who were deemed poor due to infirmities or age-related circumstances. Attitudes about the poor were wide and varied, and many divergent beliefs were held pertinent to why the poor were relegated to a life of poverty. Dating as far back as the fourteenth century religious institutions participated in alms distribution to the relief of the poor. Writing in *Poverty: A History* Bronislaw Geremek observes the following concerning OrSan Michele. "In the fourteenth century the brotherhood of OrSan Michele . . . provided partial support . . . for five to seven thousand paupers, and watched

2. Radcliffe, *Origin of the New System*, 134.

3. Radcliffe, *Origin of the New System*, 132.

4. Radcliffe, *Origin of the New System*, 133.

permanently over their welfare; in addition it saw regularly to the needs of about a thousand poor."[5]

The welfare of the poor was not always provided with empathetic or altruistic intentions. It is well documented that providing for the poor was a way to bring focus to the institutions providing the alms. It was an opportunity to showcase or publicize the pseudo-generosity of these religious entities. "Urban charitable institutions also organized alms distributions on a huge scale, particularly at the time of the annual banquet of the local brotherhood, which sought in this way to reaffirm its prestige and provide a spectacular display of its piety."[6]

For the poor, receiving alms came at a cost. To be poor and dependent upon charitable institutions allowed for the strict regulation of those who were often assigned to roles that were informative pertinent to their history. In this way, the record keeping on the poor and access to their history is a forerunner to the modern criminal justice system in the United States vis-à-vis probation and parole as a mechanism of control and monitoring of the poor.

Issa Kohler-Hausmann outlines how the modern criminal justice system in the United States serves as a receptacle or repository for the poor. Kohler-Hausmann writes, in *Misdemeanorland: Criminal Courts and Social Control in an Age of broken Windows Policing*, "Comparatively trivial infractions entangle people in the tentacles of the criminal justice system . . . and generate records that can be accessed by potential employers . . . or other important decision makers."[7]

According to Geremek this is the case with regard to the Order of San Michele. "It is clear that the main object of the exercise was to impose more rigorous controls on the poor population . . . listed in a register in which, alongside their names, various details concerning them were inscribed."[8]

5. Geremek, *Poverty: A History*, 38.
6. Geremek, *Poverty: A History*, 39.
7. Kohler-Hausmann, *Misdemeanorland*, 1.
8. Geremek, *Poverty: A History*, 39.

Paradoxically, historically to instrumentalize the poor as a constituency is an opportunity for the exploitation of the most vulnerable in our society. Whether the institutions established to oversee poor relief in medieval Europe, or institutions established to oversee the poor confined within penal institutions in the United States, dealing with the poor is to monetize their misery. Geremek writes, "It assumed that the alms collected would be pooled in a common fund . . . it did contain some forceful criticism of the abuses committed by the Church in its administration of hospitals and of the misuse of funds destined for the poor."[9]

In the United States Criminal Justice System the entrepreneurial opportunities to exploit the poor are not only in the CJ system proper; however, the many businesses that depend upon the incarcerated or the poor to profit from their confinement continues to expand. One such enterprise is the communication industry which charges exorbitant fees to place a phone call. Eric Markowitz, in an article titled "Making Profits On The Captive Prison Market," makes the following observation. "The American incarceration boom has given rise to companies that provide products and services, like phone calls for inmates, to government prisons in rather unsavory ways."[10] The business of alms giving, poor relief, or mass incarceration, too often have historically meant the capitalization of institutions to exploit the poor.

Some beliefs held were that the poor were less favored by God, and those with the good fortune of wealth were somehow favored by God, and the poor existed in order for the possessors of wealth to exercise their religious faith through aiding the poor. Other societal beliefs held were that the poor were simply lacking in fortitude and lacked the motivation to improve their lot. In an article titled "Institutional and Legal Responses to Begging in Medieval England" by Elaine Clark, the following observation is made. "Seen individually, beggars were pathetic and vulnerable . . . viewed collectively they were thought to be dangerous and willfully idle. Parliament's decision to regulate begging . . . compelled

9. Geremek, *Poverty: A History*, 201.

10. Markowitz, "Captive Prison Market," para. 1.

the king's subjects to rethink the claims of the needy . . . "[11] The nascent theory or belief that the poor constitute a potential work force, either for the redemption of the poor in one sense, or for the profitability of the larger society, were more or less prominent features of the poor problem in Europe throughout various periods of history. "Suspicious of the underserving poor, anxious officials restricted almsgiving in the later 1300s and advocated the regulation of labor. . . . Regulatory norms and a pronounced concern with discriminating charity were recurrent features of medieval life."[12]

The Poor Law Amendment Act of 1834, or New Poor Law, as it is often referred to, was a response to the growing demographic of the impoverished within Europe. Although other factors such as plagues and droughts contributed to the rise of poverty, progress and advancements in manufacturing had a debilitating effect upon the poor. Writing in "The English Poor Law of 1834 And the Cohesion of Agricultural Society," Anthony Brundage clearly identifies manufacturing as a significant factor. "The early Victorians found in the 1834 Poor Law Amendment Act a focus for many of the social and moral issues created by the onset of industrialization."[13]

The Poor Law Amendment Act was not without its critics. Many prominent opponents of the New Poor Law opposed its enactment on various grounds. One such influential critic was Thomas Robert Malthus, who wrote that the New Poor Laws would have an adverse effect on the labor market as well as wages. Writing in an article titled "Malthus and Reform of The Poor Law" Anne Digby makes the follow observation. "It is suggested that it was as a reformer, as much as an abolitionist, that Thomas Robert Malthus (1776–1834) was to influence the shaping of the new Poor Law . . . "[14] In 1803 and in 1817 Malthus wrote two significant essays in which he elaborated upon his opposing of the Poor Laws. "In these and other writings he criticized the impact which the poor Laws had on the labor market and on wages. Poor relief

11. Clark, "Institutional and Legal Responses," 447.
12. Clark, "Institutional and Legal Responses," 448.
13. Brundage, "English Poor Law," 405.
14. Digby, "Malthus and Reform," 1.

encouraged the growth of population and thus increased the supply of labor beyond demand, lowering wages."[15] Prior to the 1834 New Poor Law enactment, Europe had many iterations of policies and administration of poor relief strategies, with some more or less successful in their intent. The theories of Malthus figured prominently into the debate and shaping of the New Poor Laws. "The views of Malthus were significant in shaping the debate over poor law policy for nearly 40 years before the decisive reform of 1834."[16]

One prominent proponent of relief for the poor, and a leading voice in the fashioning of the New Poor Laws that would eventually be shaped in Europe was Jeremy Bentham, the influential philosopher and father of utilitarianism. In an article titled "Writings on the Poor Law" Michael Quinn makes the observation concerning Bentham: "He moved beyond the commonplace indictment of idleness and drink to recognize that unemployment, ill health, old age, pregnancy and childbirth constituted a standing threat to the viability of the families of the rural poor."[17] Arguably, one of the most significant recommendations made by Bentham is his advocacy that relief for the poor not be contingent upon work or labor. The reverberations of this debate are evident in our modern society today in the United States, to the extent that the ideological divide or fault line within our welfare system is the question: How should welfare and work be related? Quinn writes, "He envisaged the provision of medical care, and of ante- and post-natal services to the independent poor, and the establishment of midwifery schools in a national system of workhouses. In 'Pauper Systems Compared' . . . above all for its severance of the link between subsistence and labour."[18]

The image of the dystopian work house in popular culture during the Victorian period is etched in our collective consciousness, as we recall the Charles Dickens' character Oliver Twist,

15. Digby, "Malthus and Reform," 1.
16. Digby, "Malthus and Reform," 1.
17. Bentham, *Writings on the Poor Laws*, 359.
18. Bentham, *Writings on the Poor Laws*, 359.

imploring the house manager for more food, food of which one assumes is desirable if your lot is of the poorest of the poor. In an article titled "London, Poverty and the working classes: The Novel 1832–1880" by Ruth Richardson, the writer captures the essence of life in the work house. "Most people nowadays know about the Poor Law and its workhouses from Oliver Twist . . . The image of the skinny neglected little boy asking for more has become a classic."[19] Whatever the proximity of the work house to Dickens so to speak, his father it is reported spent time in a debtors' prison. Dickens wrote of the horrors and abuses of life in the work house. "For Charles Dickens, writing a novel about the Poor Law was a thoughtful intervention in a contemporary national debate. You can hear in his tone of voice—occasionally heavy with satire or irony—that he regarded the Poor Law as profoundly un-Christian."[20]

If the work house design was intended to discourage entrance into its facilities by the so-called able body poor, the architectural design of the work house by architect Sampson Kempthrone, is as foreboding and dystopic a design as can be imagined. What some refer to as a cruciform configuration, or reflecting the shape of the cross, the work house architecture of Kempthrone is indistinguishable from the penitentiaries of the United States.

The first penitentiary built in the United States was Eastern State Penitentiary, established circa 1829, and was designed by architect John Haviland from Britain. To the casual observer, a side-by-side pictorial view of Eastern State Penitentiary and Sampson Kempthrone's work house, the two buildings reflect identical characteristics. Peter Higginbotham, writing in *The Workhouse in Berkshire* describes the Abingdon Union Work House. "The Abingdon Union workhouse was designed by the PLC commissioned architect Sampson Kempthrone . . . based on American prison designs. The high plain walls and rows of small windows reinforced the severe visual effect."[21] The concern with the architecture of work houses, or penitentiaries, is not only a question of

19. Richardson, "Oliver Twist and the work house," 1.
20. Richardson, "Oliver Twist and the work house," 1.
21. Higginbotham, "The Workhouse in Berkshire."

aesthetics; however, the impact on the psychological debilitation of its residents is punitive. In an article titled, "Is There Such a Thing as 'Good' Prison Design" by Rachael Slade, the following observation is made. "Some would argue that America's prison problem is very much a design problem. Facilities are usually built like fortresses—monoliths in rural location . . . and concrete block which mercilessly reflect the endless noise inside prisons . . . "[22] This is the architectural model informing Sampson Kempthrone's work house in 1835, home to women and children, mentally ill, and elderly, and able-bodied men who were potential predators, upon the vulnerably poor housed in these castles of despair and misery. The work house of Europe or the penitentiary in the United States may as well have been designed by Dante Alighieri.

III. Work House

The workhouses of Europe, like the penal system in the United States, evolved and at various points in the history of each institution respectively, attempted to define its role as either a punitive institution or a rehabilitation institution. In both cases, the former has been the dominant characteristic of each. In Europe, the work house was an infamous destination for the poor and was the last place any individual or family would want to enter as a last resort. The work house was intended to serve as a deterrent in the sense that it was harsh and inhumane. On the other hand the work house did provide free education for children along with medical attention. Despite the unintended benefits the work houses of Europe were notorious. "The gates of a workhouse in Hamburg bore the message: Labore nutrior, labore plector (By work I am nourished, by work I am punished). A similar notice, at the entrance to a workhouse in Dessau, read: Miseris et Malis (For the Poor and the Wicked)."[23]

---

22. Slade, "'Good' Prison Design?," para. 2.

23. Geremek, *Poverty: A History*, 215.

History is replete with tragic accounts of individuals who survived, suffered, or died in the custody of workhouses. The case of Edward Cooper is one such case that has come to light, however, in no way an isolated incident. Edward Cooper was starved to death while in the custody of a workhouse known as Isle of Wight Union. In an article titled, "Where is the Fault?: The Starvation of Edward Cooper at the Isle of Wight Workhouse in 1877" by Kim Price, Price chronicles the demise of Cooper. "Edward Cooper was a disabled pauper who died of starvation in a workhouse 'idiot' ward. His neglect was the result of systemic problems, exacerbated by policy, and the poor law's free market approach to employing doctors in this period."[24] In the case of Edward Cooper, referred to as representative of the so-called deserving poor, as opposed to the able-bodied poor, he was caught and lost in a system that indiscriminately despised and neglected its poor.

Though Cooper is a case that surfaced and is emblematic of the dereliction of the workhouse, it does not take much imagination to comprehend the magnitude or scope of widespread abuse in the workhouse, of those who remain anonymous. "The Coopers were the 'deserving poor' and should have received the cream of charity and voluntary aid. Instead, they slipped through the gaping holes of a welfare net stretched wide by recession and the withdrawal of outdoor relief."[25]

Like the penal institutions within the United States, which have become the *de facto* mentally ill asylums, due to decades of legislation discriminating against the mentally ill poor, workhouses in Europe housed the mentally ill and those misdiagnosed as being mentally ill, with disastrous results. In an article titled "Lunatic Asylum in the Workhouse: St. Peter's Hospital, Bristol, 1698–1861," Leonard Smith details some of the deficiencies at Bristol. "Under the old Poor Law; 'St Peter's Hospital' was opened in 1698. . . . It's clientele included 'lunatics' and 'idiots.' . . . Its many

24. Price, "'Where is the Fault?,'" 21.
25. Price, "'Where is the Fault?,'" 21.

deficiencies brought condemnation in the national survey of provision for the insane in 1844."[26]

IV. Context / Conditions / History Leading to Creation of Mass Incarceration

The legacy of Africans in America, or Africans in the Diaspora, as black people are often referred to, is a fitting description which informs observers that the tragedy of slavery in the United States, and therefore the characterization of these once proud people as slaves, is only a fraction of their story. The context and the history of African Americans leading to mass incarceration must be understood as a protracted, intentional, and systematic effort by the founders of the United States, to marginalize and control an entire cultural population of people. At times the marginalization was for free labor, and at other times black people were marginalized in order to maintain control of a population newly emancipated, and eventually to impede this population from progressing politically, educationally, and socially.

The intentional effort to marginalize and suppress an entire population has been at the expense of the nation itself in terms of development. It is no coincidence that in the United States, particularly southern states such as Mississippi, Alabama, Georgia, and others, are perennially at the bottom when ranked for public school performance and test scores.

Thomas Sowell, an economist at the Hoover Institution, and author of *Wealth, Poverty And Politics* suggests there is correlative evidence for this phenomenon. "A society which arbitrarily restricts the education or employment of women, for example can forfeit half the human capital potential of its own population. . . . The skills forfeited in this way have ranged from clock-making to nuclear physics."[27]

---

26. Smith, "Lunatic Asylum," 225.

27. Sowell, *Wealth, Poverty and Politics*, 159–60.

Such is the case of Vivien Theodore Thomas, born in 1910 and despite segregation and all of its debilitating social norms, went on to make significant contributions in the field of medicine, most notably at Johns Hopkins Hospital in Baltimore, Maryland. During the era of Jim Crow segregation much of the work of Vivien Thomas went unacknowledged until many years later, when Johns Hopkins awarded Thomas an honorary doctoral degree, and HBO produced a major production highlighting his life titled *Something the Lord Made*. Writing in *Journal of Medical Biography* by Erdinc Soylu, Thanos Athanasiou, and Omar A. Jarral, in an article titled "Vivian Theodore Thomas (1910–1985)," the following observation is made: "He overcame challenging personal circumstances to become an innovator in pediatric cardiac surgery, despite having no formal college education. He played an important role in assisting Alfred Blalock and Helen Taussig in the development of the 'Blalock-Taussig' shunt . . . "[28]

Where are the Vivien Theodore Thomas inventors today? They are incarcerated! How much genius has been lost in either United States penitentiaries or the work houses of Europe? In the United States context the Jim Crow era was marked by domestic terrorism and arguably worse than slavery. Following the Reconstruction period from 1865 through 1875, when African Americans made historic progress in everything from banking to education, there was a backlash by white America that has debilitated the African American to this date. The systematic destruction of African American life and the pathologies of substance abuse, fatherless homes, failure in education, and unprecedented mass incarceration all have their roots in slavery and Jim Crow.

The phenomenon of lynching was the method most often employed to maintain African Americans as an underclass. From vigilante lynch mobs to the theology of white Protestantism, the theory of black inferiority and white superiority permeated every aspect of society.

James Cone in *The Cross and The Lynching Tree* writes, "I was born in Arkansas, a lynching state. . . . White people were virtually

28. Soylu et al., "Vivien Theodore Thomas," 1.

free to do anything to blacks with impunity. The violent crosses of the Ku Klux Klan . . . and white racists preached a dehumanizing segregated gospel . . . every Sunday."[29] This is the context of the last 150 years that has shaped the African American experience. Put another way, African Americans are only thirteen generations of high school graduating classes removed from slavery. This is the context and these are the conditions, that have led to the impoverishment of a significant segment of the African American community, and the introduction to mass incarceration.

V. Prison Industrial Complex

Mass incarceration, the prison industrial complex, or the warehousing of African Americans, began in earnest immediately following the Emancipation Proclamation bringing an end to the enslavement of African Americans. The institution of slavery, among other things, was a means of free labor for not only the South, but the country as a whole benefited from the revenue of slavery. With the end of slavery the southern states had to replace its free source of labor. The Convict Lease System was the new way of supplying free labor to the South for the railroad industry, mining, agriculture, and other labor-intensive jobs. The state of Alabama in 1866 under Governor Robert M. Patton leased the inmates housed at the penitentiary for labor in and around the state of Alabama. For a fee charged to the particular business enterprise by the state it would provide free inmate labor. The Convict Lease System became the new source of free labor for southern states, and was a lucrative incentive to incarcerate newly freed former slaves. It is the Convict Lease System that is the forerunner of the contemporary for-profit prison system.

Thorsten Sellin writing in *Slavery and the Penal System* makes the following observation. "In 1866, the governor of Alabama leased the penitentiary to a contractor who was charged the sum of five dollars and given a loan. The legislature granted him

---

29. Cone, *The Cross and the Lynching Tree*, xv.

permission to work the prisoners outside the walls; they were soon found in the Ironton and New Castle mines."[30]

The incarceration of African Americans reached epidemic proportions during the administration of then President William Jefferson Clinton, as a result of the so-called "war on drugs," which focused government resources on arresting low-level street drug users and sellers. Insidious laws such as "Three Strikes Law" passed in 1994 imposed harsh sentences, often life sentences for menial crimes for repeat offenders. These laws, and the crack addiction plaguing African American communities, almost eradicated an entire generation of young black men and swelled the penitentiaries across the United States. Historically, addiction in the African American community has been referred to the criminal court system, in contrast to the opioid epidemic more likely to affect the white populous, and treated as a medical epidemic with sympathetic drug courts. With a ready population of incarcerated African Americans and often poor white Americans, the criminal justice penal system is able to utilize this labor pool to contribute to its state revenue. A news release by the State of Maryland, Department of Public Safety and Correctional Services of 2005 boasts the following. "In fiscal year '05 the former State Use Industries had revenues of just under $40 million, profits of $2 million, and a record 1,530 inmate workers. Since June 2002, the division has transferred $8 million to the state's General Fund."

VI. Institutions for Social Control

In an ironic, perhaps cruel theological twist of fate, one of the largest population of churches for African American males, is located within the confines of the penitentiaries across the United States. This does not only hold true concerning the Christian faith, however; the Islamic faith boasts a large contingent of black men practicing their faith.

---

30. Sellin, *Slavery and the Penal System*, 150–51.

A concern for future investigation may be the research focusing upon the question of how emerging theology is informed within the context of the prison culture or jail milieu, then reintroduced into black communities upon release of ex-offenders. Often, this theological formation can be, however not always, informed by exaggerated masculinity and dominance, or worse, misogyny.

The work house of Europe and the prison industrial complex of the United States are, and have been historically, used as institutions for social control of the poor and marginalized of their respective societies. Both the work house and the prison industrial complex share a similar history from architecture to violent control of its residents. Moreover, the threat of placement in either of these social control institutions had, and in the United States has, a debilitating effect on the communities, and a horrific scar on the psyche of African Americans and descendants of European work houses.

CHAPTER 8

The Sunday-School Society and Poverty Relief as Pedagogy in Contemporary Blighted African American Urban Communities

THE GOALS AND CATECHESIS of William Fox, Esq., and the Sunday-School Society of the early nineteenth century, are instructional as pedagogy for poverty eradication in blighted African American urban communities in the twenty-first century.

In the first half of the nineteenth century circa 1831, William Fox witnessed the grinding poverty that afflicted the poor in England, as he traveled throughout certain regions of the country. Fox described conditions which he witnessed simply as deplorable. "The wholesale line of business in which Mr. Fox had now engaged required him to take frequent journeys through the several counties of England, which afforded him opportunities of witnessing the deplorable ignorance of the lower classes of our population."[1]

William Fox found it untenable that a country that identified as a religious country, a Christian state, could live with the coexistence and the contradiction of religious faith and poverty to the

---

1. Ivimey, *Memoir of William Fox*, 15.

extent it existed in various parts of England. "Could it have been imagined that in a Christian country, a Protestant country too, no provision would be made for the education of poor children . . . "[2] Here, Fox presages the mass exodus or *white flight*, from urban inner-city schools to alternative private education, leaving public school education as the *de facto* domain of poor people in the United States. One of the most extreme examples of this is the Eager Street Academy, located in Baltimore City, and housed within the Maryland Department of Corrections.

Fox was not only concerned over the immediate conditions of the poor; however, he was perceptive enough to understand that this type of impoverished condition threatened generations to follow. Without the alleviation of the pathologies that ensnared these identified populations as a result of poverty, Fox feared that the impending moral decline would be entrenched and intractable. Addressing the concern of the children of the poor, Fox makes this insightful observation: "In places where extensive manufactories are established . . . when they grow up they are therefore found in the greatest ignorance with respect to religion and morality . . . it becomes the inheritance of their posterity, and is entailed from generation to generation."[3]

It is remarkable that what William Fox observed in the early nineteenth century, is the state of affairs as it relates to blighted African American urban communities in the twenty-first century. The trajectory of African American males from impoverished urban centers, to jails and prisons in the United States today, is traceable to the failure of a dysfunctional education system, as well as a loss of basic moral bearings pertinent to family cohesiveness among other variables.

Caroline Wolf Harlow writing in an article titled "Education and Correctional Populations," makes the following observation. "About 41% of inmates in the Nation's State and Federal prisons and local jails in 1997 and 31% of probationers had not completed high school or its equivalent. In comparison, 18% of the general

2. Ivimey, *Memoir of William Fox*, 18.
3. Ivimey, *Memoir of William Fox*, 38.

population age 18 or older had not finished the 12th grade."[4] What William Fox feared has become a social epidemic in blighted African American urban communities, despite the fact that Fox's context was nineteenth-century England.

William Fox without the benefit of data and statistical analysis, or longitudinal study and research methods, clearly understood that religious education was the method through which poverty would be breached. "Whether some plan might not be adopted by which all the children of the poor might receive a scriptural education, by being taught to read the Bible."[5] William Fox's benevolence extended beyond literacy, and into the concern of social welfare for the poor of England. "He accordingly not only clothed all the poor people of the parish, men, women, and children, but set up a daily school for the free instruction of all who were willing to attend it. In this school the reading was entirely confined to the Bible . . . "[6]

Introducing the poor to literacy through the reading of the Bible and religious instruction, William Fox either inadvertently or serendipitously provided a way for the poor to not only learn religion but to gain greater insights in general. Writing for the Pew Research Center the following observation is made. "Religion and education, two of humankind's most ancient endeavors have long had a close relationship. Historians and social scientists have written about this relationship and about how the two may influence each other."[7] William Fox clearly intended that religious education not only serve for the benefit of the afterlife of the poor as some critics contend; however, that religious education would be instructive for their present condition. "To promote the extensive influence and advantage of such schools—to give the children an opportunity of knowing what the sacred oracles contain—and, above all, to rescue them from low habits of vice and idleness, and

4. US Department of Justice, *Education and Correctional Populations*, 1.

5. Ivimey, *Memoir of William Fox*, 16.

6. Ivimey, *Memoir of William Fox*, 16.

7. Pew Research Center, "Religion and Education," 115.

to initiate them into a moral and religious course of life, are the ends herein proposed."[8]

The goals and catechesis of William Fox and the Sunday-School Society are instructional for poverty eradication in blighted African American urban communities today. In an article titled "Effects of Religious Practice on Education," we can identify the accomplishment of the goals of the Sunday-School Society present in this claim. "For youth in impoverished neighborhoods, religious attendance made the greatest difference in academic achievement prospects. . . . As rates of unemployment, poverty, and female-headed households grew in a neighborhood, the impact of a student's level of religious practice on academic progress became even stronger."[9]

Fox understood the importance of the familial or social milieu of children in poverty. For Fox, creating an environment that served as a healthy surrogate for children, which then created structure is evident in his writings in *The Sunday-School Society*. "Enter his cottage, and you will see the indigent pair dealing out to their children their scanty allowance: bread and water are frequently all their fare, and it would pierce a heart of stone to hear them crying for more. . . . Their clothing also bears the mark of extreme indigence . . . "[10]

Fox's highlighting of the poor families living conditions suggests that he was insightful as to the effects of poverty as a debilitating source. Clearly, this focus extends beyond the concern of the spiritual condition of the poor and seeks a corrective for their social conditions. By creating a Sunday-School Society, William Fox was restructuring the environment in which poor children lived. In blighted African American urban communities, where progressive religious instruction exists, the intentions of the Sunday-School Society are replicated in an effort to create a stable learning environment and social milieu. "Surrounded by adults and peers who care about worthy accomplishments, religiously

8. Ivimey, *Memoir of William Fox*, 39.

9. Marripedia, "Effects of Religious Practice," 9.

10. Ivimey, *Memoir of William Fox*, 18.

involved youth tend to score higher than other adolescents on school achievement, social success, confidence in self, and [parents report of their] personal maturity . . . "[11]

The goals and catechesis of William Fox and the Sunday-School Society of the nineteenth century are instructional for poverty eradication in blighted African American urban communities in the twenty-first century for a number of reasons. The effects of poverty are similar in both early England as well as modern urban African American communities. Poverty and ignorance are intertwined. William Fox understood that through literacy and moral teaching the grip of poverty could be lessened. Fox understands that poverty has implications for family instability, educational underachievement, reduces vocational choices, and plays a significant role in morally healthy or unhealthy decision making. In the urban African American context the breakdown in moral codes coincides with an increase in HIV and AIDS, intravenous drug use, single parent homes which decreases earning potential, increased incarceration, violence upon women, uptick in homicides, and other pathologies of blighted urban life.

William Fox and the Sunday-School Society understood what many highly functional societies understood. Two such societies are noteworthy here. The Jewish community placed significant emphasis upon passing on learning from generation to generation. " . . . Throughout the first millennium, no people other than the Jews had a norm requiring fathers to educate their sons. This religious obligation meant that male Jews, to a greater degree than their contemporaries, were literate, which gave them an advantage in commerce and trade."[12] Also, Hinduism places an even higher emphasis upon learning and suggests that learning is the building block upon which life should be built. "Learning is the foundational stage in the Hindu scheme of what constitutes a good and a meaningful life, Rambachan says. Since ignorance is regarded as a

---

11. Marripedia, "Effects of Religious Practice," 8.

12. Marripedia, "Effects of Religious Practice," 6.

source of human suffering, he adds, the solution to the problem of ignorance is knowledge or learning."[13]

William Fox and the Sunday-School Society were pioneers in the religious education of the poor, and therefore consequently, early workers toward the eradication of poverty, which now serves as a blueprint for poverty relief in contemporary blighted African American urban communities.

13. Pew Research Center, "Religion and Education," 122.

CHAPTER 9

The Unethical Corrupting
of Law and Order in Conversation
with Dietrich Bonhoeffer

DIETRICH BONHOEFFER WAS BORN in 1906 in Breslav, Germany, preceding the rise of Adolf Hitler as Chancellor by only twenty-seven years in 1933. The proximity between Dietrich Bonhoeffer and Adolf Hitler in Germany during this time would significantly inform Bonhoeffer's ethics and theology. Much of Dietrich Bonhoeffer's writings are in the context of refuting the nationalistic Aryan supremacy propaganda permeating German religious and political thinking in the early twentieth century.

When Bonhoeffer's ethics and theology are considered in the proper context, they illuminate the construct of truth within the opaque disinformation of Nazi Germany. The concept of truth, or telling the truth, or acting in a truthful manner, has been the subject of ethical interpretation of ethicists and philosophers from John Stuart Mill reflected in consequentialism, to Immanuel Kant reflected in deontologism. Bonhoeffer's essay, "What Does It Mean to Tell the Truth?" illuminates with clarity the essence of truth telling and its limitations and possibilities bound by context. Bonhoeffer's ethic in this context unencumbers the ethicist or religious leader of unnecessary and distracting impediments, of presupposed and contrived pseudo-ethical paradigms and ideals, often imposed from the opposition.

Dietrich Bonhoeffer, unlike many of the liberation theologians such as Martin Luther King Jr., or Gustavo Gutierrez, was not born into a family representative of the underclass or minority class. Arguably, Bonhoeffer's social location in German society from a cultured and solidly middle class family milieu is what is at once endearing and improbable pertinent to his response to Nazism.

Given Bonhoeffer's pedigree he could have been an accomplished professional in any number of vocations. Bonhoeffer is identified as a very good musician throughout much of the biographical depictions profiling his life, and suggests that his early orientation gave no hints of the resistance theologian he would become. Writing in *Theologian of Resistance: The Life and Thought of Dietrich Bonhoeffer*, Christiane Tietz makes the following observation. "Like many of those Germans who would join the political conspiracy to overthrow the National Socialist regime, Dietrich Bonhoeffer came from a middle-class family. His father, Karl Bonhoeffer, was professor of psychiatry and neurology, first in Breslau (what is today Wroclaw, Poland) and then after 1912 at the Charite Hospital in Berlin."[1]

Although Dietrich Bonhoeffer was influenced by and nurtured in an environment that facilitated his intellectualism and growth as a self-actualized person, this environment did not necessarily come from the church, of which the Bonhoeffer family was not strongly involved. Christiane Tietz observes, "The family was surprised when Dietrich Bonhoeffer decided to study theology, since the institutional church played hardly any role in their everyday lives."[2] What the Bonhoeffer family could not have anticipated was that the zeitgeist would place Dietrich Bonhoeffer as a leader in the church resistance movement against the Third Reich, Aryan

1. Tietz, *Theologian of Resistance*, 1.
2. Tietz, *Theologian of Resistance*, 5.

supremacy, the Aryan Paragraph, and finally call Bonhoeffer to martyrdom.

Christiane Tietz makes the following observation of Bonhoeffer's father. "Later, when the Church Struggle reached its most intensive phase, he wrote his son that he feared that a quiet, uneventful pastor's life . . . would really be almost a pity for you. So far as uneventfulness is concerned, I was greatly mistaken."[3]

This is both the context and the backdrop necessary to gain insight into the ethics and theology of Dietrich Bonhoeffer. It is in this context that Bonhoeffer developed his ethic and theological thought as it relates to identifying truth, truth telling, and the myriad concerns informing a pedagogy of truth.

It would seem logical to begin with a discussion relative to truth, what truth is, or telling the truth. When we begin with a discussion of a lie in its historical, destructive, insidious, and vile cultural context and how it has been a destructive evil in the history of humanity, it is then that we identify the urgency for and of truth to rescue humanity.

One of the contrived pseudo-ethical paradigms evil states and governments often establish, is under the guise of law and order. It is under such law and order pseudo-ethical paradigms that the apartheid system in South Africa maintained supporters around the world. It is the same pseudo-ethical paradigm of law and order that facilitated Jim Crow laws, and allowed them to endure for so long because of its disguise of law and order.

It is the same disguise that Hannah Arendt referred to as the banality of evil. Writing in *Eichmann in Jerusalem: A Report on the Banality of Evil* Arendt observed the following. "Arendt found Eichmann an ordinary, rather bland, bureaucrat, who in her words, was neither perverted nor sadistic, but terrifyingly normal. . . . Instead, he performed evil deeds without evil intentions, a fact connected to his thoughtlessness, a disengagement from the reality of his evil acts."[4] Adolf Eichmann was simply following orders, a claim that has found resonance with law and order adherents.

---

3. Tietz, *Theologian of Resistance*, 5.

4. White, "What Did Hannah Arendt Really Mean?," para. 2.

It is here that Dietrich Bonhoeffer's ethics help to remove the veil and to expose the lie of law and order in its worst context. Clifford Green and Michael DeJonge observe in *The Bonhoeffer Reader* what Bonhoeffer refers to as Satan's truth. "There is such a thing as Satan's truth. Its nature is to deny everything real under the guise of the truth. It feeds on hatred against the real, against the world created and loved by God. It gives the impression of carrying out God's judgment on the fall of the real into sin. But God's truth judges what is created out of love; Satan's truth judges what is created out of envy and hatred."[5]

Although there appears to be a contradiction in Bonhoeffer on this point, nonetheless, his characterization of Satan's truth is invaluable. The contradiction is that Satan and truth are irreconcilable. Green and DeJonge write in *The Bonhoeffer Reader*: "These reflections lead to the recognition that the essence of lying is found much deeper than in the contradiction between thought and speech. We could say that the person who stands behind what is said makes it into a lie or the truth."[6]

There are times historically when the body politic is constitutionally a lie. Dietrich Bonhoeffer was confronted with such a body politic as was the case in Nazi Germany. Or, stated another way, Aryan supremacy was Satan's truth of superiority referencing the Jewish culture and people. In this context the person in Bonhoeffer's statement is the body politic, the person standing behind what is said by Bonhoeffer's analogy is congenitally corrupted, therefore all laws emanating from the body politic are without the possibility of redemption, and must be refuted even if they are cloaked in the lie of the German Evangelical Church (German Christians), or other state sponsored institutions. Bonhoeffer realized, as did Henry David Thoreau, Mahatma Gandhi, and Martin Luther King Jr., that there is no moral or ethical requirement to answer the state in a corresponding manner consistent with or conforming to Satan's truth.

5. Bonhoeffer, *The Bonhoeffer Reader*, 752.
6. Bonhoeffer, *The Bonhoeffer Reader*, 754.

Those seeking truth through social justice have no moral obligation to conform to Bonhoeffer's characterization of Satan's truth, nor to be in compliance with laws that dehumanize or devalue life. There is no more obligation to conform than there is for the child referred to by Dietrich Bonhoeffer to answer an unjust teacher who disregards the appropriate boundaries. "When the various orders of life no longer respect one another, then words become untrue. For example, a teacher asks a child in front of the class whether it is true that the child's father often comes home drunk. . . . To be sure, the child perceives that this question is an unjustified invasion into the order of the family and must be warded off."[7]

When the social contract impedes, or is an unjustified invasion into the order as Bonhoeffer suggests, and the realization of individuals or communities to live into the abundant life as identified by Jesus Christ, there exists a moral imperative to resist the unjust laws, lies, that conspire to marginalize those affected by their enactment. Writing in *Doing Christian Ethics from the Margins*, Miguel A. De La Torre makes the following observation. "Unfortunately those who control the instruments of social power claim a monopoly on truth to the detriment of the disenfranchised. . . . Their control of taxation, judiciary, and the armed forces gives them free access to all political processes."[8]

Telling the truth, or being in compliance, can be understood as adhering to the laws of the land by its citizenry in the context of the majority, or those who make up the dominant demographic. However, as Bonhoeffer illuminates, telling the truth is dynamic as opposed to static, and can often be understood differently from below or from the underclass perspective. Bonhoeffer states, " . . . From this we can see immediately that "telling the truth" means different things, depending on where one finds oneself. The relevant relationship must be taken into account."[9]

---

7. Bonhoeffer, *The Bonhoeffer Reader*, 753.

8. De La Torre, *Christian Ethics from the Margins*, 15.

9. Bonhoeffer, *The Bonhoeffer Reader*, 750.

Bonhoeffer's interpretation of truth in this context gives him a certain vulnerability to critics who might suggest that his understanding of truth is one of convenience. There is a pseudo-ethical paradigm which purports that truth at all costs is virtuous and must disregard context. By being vulnerable to criticism of his ethical hermeneutic of truth, it is here that Bonhoeffer demonstrates moral courage through his concern of tangible reality, and not abstract ethical morality. "The truthfulness of our words that we owe God must take on concrete form in the world. Our word should be truthful not in principle but concretely. A truthfulness that is not concrete is not truthful at all before God."[10]

It is evident that Bonhoeffer's experience as part of the resistance against Aryan doctrine provided the concreteness to which he refers to. This concreteness provides a solidarity with oppressed people around the world, and makes Bonhoeffer's ethics clearly identifiable with the marginalized. There is a kind of satisfaction in Bonhoeffer's ethics here, that is experienced for example, when a law or ruling is passed down from a high court which is not true and impactful in the abstract only, but also in the concrete or real world where people's lives are impacted.

Dietrich Bonhoeffer lived in a historical period which required him to confront evil institutions in a manner most ethicists will only know theoretically. Any critique of Bonhoeffer's ethics must be applied with a measure of gravity and sensitivity to his context. Bonhoeffer concludes his interpretation of what constitutes a lie by somewhat of a concession. It is a concession that can only be appreciated when viewed through the context of history. Bonhoeffer places the behavior of lying in perspective: "If one characterizes this sort of behavior as a lie, then lying receives a moral consecration and justification that contradicts its meaning in every respect."[11] Bonhoeffer's ethical reasoning negates superficial, pseudo-ethical paradigms that appeal to rigid legalistic moralists, and disentangles all those who love freedom from the yoke of contrived unreasonable moral obligations.

10. Bonhoeffer, *The Bonhoeffer Reader*, 750.

11. Bonhoeffer, *The Bonhoeffer Reader*, 754.

CHAPTER 10

Dietrich Bonhoeffer
and God's Revelation

I. Introduction

DIETRICH BONHOEFFER EXPERIENCES GOD's revelation in his final
years confined to a prison institution. In a way that was elusive during his freedom, he finds solidarity with "The Crucified People" of
the world, to include "Black people of the cross," as depicted in *The
Cross and The Lynching Tree* emerging in the work of James Cone.
In this revelation an envisioned church more reminiscent of Jesus
of the Gospels emerges. "It remains an experience of incomparable
value that we have for once learned to see the great events of world
history from below, from the perspective of the outcasts . . . the oppressed . . . from the perspective of the suffering."[1] W. E. B. Du Bois,
the first African American to earn a PhD at Harvard University,
clearly understood the connection Bonhoeffer is making between
the value of seeing history from below, and the revelation of God
in suffering people. Du Bois writes, "Yet Jesus Christ . . . was poor
and we are poor. . . . He was persecuted and crucified, and we are

1. Barnett, "*After Ten Years*", 30.

mobbed and lynched. If Jesus Christ came to America He would associate with negroes and Italians and working people . . . "[2]

It is in the context of Bonhoeffer's prison confinement that the social milieu of the poor and the oppressed, the Crucified People of the world, is experienced firsthand in a manner that cannot be replicated through simulation or academic exercises, whereby one has agency to step in and out of the simulation of impoverished conditions at will. People from positions of power have often attempted to simulate social conditions, often with good intentions, however, with the reality that they have the agency and the power, to move in and out of context at will. Henry David Thoreau, in *Life in the Woods*, is such an example.

Miguel A. De La Torre, writing in *Doing Christian Ethics from the Margins*, refers to "Organic Intellectuals." "These ministers and scholars attempt to learn from the disenfranchised while serving them as organic intellectuals (to borrow a term from Antonio Gramsci) . . . intellectuals grounded in the social reality of the marginalized . . . "[3] Bonhoeffer becomes an organic participant, albeit not by his choosing, in the most authentic way possible. As a result, Bonhoeffer experiences the social milieu of the Crucified People by experiencing loss of freedom, loss of agency, loss of power or powerless, loss of social capital, and loss of identity, thus experiencing God's revelation through suffering as articulated in *Letters and Papers from Prison*.

II. The Realities of People Living Below or in the Margins: Dietrich Bonhoeffer and Revelation Through Suffering

The experience of loss has been a central and constant motif of African Americans in the United States. The renowned African American sociologist, William Julius Wilson, once described poverty in America as the lack of choices. The perpetually impoverished

---

2. Cone, *The Cross and the Lynching Tree*, 103.

3. De La Torre, *Christian Ethics from the Margins*, xii.

station of the Crucified People and the Lynched People in America has been one lacking in choices. The systematic disenfranchisement of an entire culture of people has been deliberate and effective. This disenfranchisement has meant the loss of freedom, loss of agency, loss of power, loss of social capital, and loss of identity.

This disenfranchisement has been codified throughout American history. In 1857, the Dred Scott decision declared that black people were not fully recognized as citizens. Additionally, Plessy v. Ferguson created and maintained the American apartheid system. Further, black people were marginalized as they lacked access to voting privileges. This right would not be granted fully until the Voting Rights Act of 1965. And, as recently as 1994, the Violent Crime Control and Law Enforcement Act, better known as the Three Strikes law, all served as systemic means of white hegemony over black people. The result has been the emasculating of African American males in particular, and African American culture in general. It is in this context that black religion and theology have been informed.

For cultures and people who are not indigenous to the African American experience, it is no small wonder that there exists a lack of understanding, lack of appreciation, as well as a lack of taking black theology or liberation theology seriously, in the manner of Western theology or theologians such as Karl Barth.

The assault on the freedoms of the Lynched People has been long and protracted as well as effective. It is not surprising then that African Americans often experience dissonance between their faith and Western Christianity. There needs to be a theology that gives voice to the context of the disenfranchisement of the Lynched People. "Black suffering needs radical and creative voices, prophetic advocates who can tell brutal and beautiful stories of how oppressed black people survived with a measure of dignity when they were not meant to."[4]

It is only through the revelation of deprivation that Bonhoeffer is able to state that the church is benefited from interpreting world history from below. As one from a prominent upbringing

---

4. Cone, *The Cross and the Lynching Tree*, 95.

and well-educated background, Bonhoeffer certainly would have been inoculated from the most severe form of human deprivation suffered by others. While one is able to be empathetic with those who exist and experience life from below, it is quite another thing to internalize and live the life of daily assaults upon one's personhood. Through his own suffering Bonhoeffer becomes one of the Crucified People, one of the Lynched People. Bonhoeffer through his incarceration and thereby the removal of his freedoms, his emasculation, understands what it is to be an African American.

Bonhoeffer describes the experiences of the Crucified People, or the Lynched People in the United States, in the most recognizable and authentic voice of oppressed people, capturing what life has been for them in North America since 1619. Bonhoeffer's context experiencing suffering in Germany under the totalitarian rule of Adolf Hitler, the genocide of Jewish people, his imprisonment and impending execution, bring him into solidarity with the Crucified People and their experiences, as well as the revelation of God, as interpreted by the oppressed people of the world. "Have there ever been people in history who in their time, like us, had so little ground under their feet, people to whom every possible alternative open to them at the time appeared equally unbearable, senseless, and contrary to life?"[5]

Through God's revelation, illuminated through the prison cell for Bonhoeffer, he was able to see and comprehend what James Cone says that Reinhold Niebuhr was unable to see or comprehend. Writing in *The Cross and the Lynching Tree*, Cone makes the observation pertinent to Niebuhr. "Niebuhr had 'eyes to see' black suffering, but I believe he lacked the 'heart to feel' it as his own . . . the problem of race was never one of his central theological or political concerns."[6] Through his suffering, confinement, and execution, Bonhoeffer gained the credibility of authenticity alongside theologians as the Reverend Dr. Martin Luther King Jr. and Archbishop Oscar Romero.

5. Bonhoeffer, *The Bonhoeffer Reader*, 762.
6. Cone, *The Cross and the Lynching Tree*, 41.

God's revelation to Bonhoeffer made discernible through confinement and suffering, places him in solidarity with the Lynched People of the Jim Crow South, as well as the crucified Jesus of Nazareth. "There was, however, an important difference between Reinhold Niebuhr and Martin Luther King Jr. that partly accounts for why King became a martyr in the civil rights movement while Niebuhr remained safely confined in his office at Union Seminary . . . "[7]

There can never be an authentic voice, as with Bonhoeffer, that resonates with the Crucified People, or the Lynched People, as long as those theologians retain freedom, agency, power, social capital, and their identity as part of the dominant culture experiencing life and theology from above. "As long as the religious leaders of . . . the dominant culture continue to construct ethical perspectives from within their cultural space of wealth and power, the marginalized will need an alternate format by which to . . . do ethics."[8] Bonhoeffer was able to develop an ethic that reflected the view from below.

Bonhoeffer was concerned with a church in Germany that excluded those who were not from German extraction, and Cone was concerned with a church in America that sanctioned Jim Crow lynching. James Cone and Dietrich Bonhoeffer were confounded by the corrupting of the church by evildoers. In either context, Germany under Hitler or lynching under Jim Crow, the church was one of the institutions that sanctioned and presided over the perverting of religion and ethics. Bonhoeffer observed, "The huge masquerade of evil has thrown all ethical concepts into confusion. That evil should appear in the form of light, good deeds, historical necessity, social justice is absolutely bewildering for one coming from the world of ethical concepts that we have received."[9] Of the Christian church and its role in the genocide of Lynched People, Cone observed, " . . . Not all crosses were liberating and loving, even when Jesus' name was invoked. White ministers sometimes

7. Cone, *The Cross and the Lynching Tree*, 71.

8. De La Torre, *Christian Ethics from the Margins*, 5.

9. Bonhoeffer, *The Bonhoeffer Reader*, 763.

served as mob leaders, blessing lynchings, or citing the stories of Ham and Cain to justify white supremacy as divine right."[10]

It was not only the so-called evil doers, however, the well-intended believers that both Bonhoeffer and Martin Luther King had to address in their challenge to the church and the state. Bonhoeffer observed, "The failure of the 'reasonable ones'—those who think, with the best of intentions and in their naïve misreading of reality, that with a bit of reason they can patch up a structure that has come out of joint—is apparent."[11] The established church, or the church that enjoys the status of a prominent social location in society, is the church that needs to be challenged due to its loss of vision and inability to view society from below. Dr. King observed, "We will have to repent in this generation not merely for the vitriolic words and actions of the bad people, but for the appalling silence of the good people."[12]

III. Conclusion

In the end, Bonhoeffer, like many who live in the margins, through revelation was able to discern what many Lynched People and Crucified People see clearly, that contrived values and value systems of those from above, are often in conflict with the values and value systems of those from below, and they are often determined in order to codify draconian laws and practices, that normalize and make virtuous hegemonic ethics and mores. It is more important to have freedom and personhood, and this often calls those from below to be in conflict with the respected dominant culture.

Bonhoeffer noted, "There is the one who determines to take a stand in the world by acting on his own freedom. He values the necessary action more highly than an untarnished conscience and reputation. He is prepared to sacrifice a barren principle to a

---

10. Cone, *The Cross and the Lynching Tree*, 76.
11. Bonhoeffer, *The Bonhoeffer Reader*, 763.
12. King Jr., *A Testament of Hope*, 296.

fruitful compromise or a barren wisdom of mediocrity to fruitful radicalism."[13]

Author Miguel A. De La Torre perhaps captures the above sentiment best when describing how his mother, one living from below, had to decide between telling the truth or telling a lie in order to qualify for employment in America as an immigrant. "Yet, the moral reasoning she employed enabled her to surmount societal structures fundamentally averse to her very existence. Which is more ethical . . . doing what needs to be done to get the job, or letting the sins of others force us to live on the streets?"[14]

The ability to suffer and identify with those who live from below, the Crucified People, the Lynched People, enables the church to more readily resemble the church Jesus envisioned, and served as revelation for Dietrich Bonhoeffer through the cell of a prison.

13. Bonhoeffer, *The Bonhoeffer Reader*, 764.
14. De La Torre, *Christian Ethics from the Margins*, 22.

CHAPTER 11

Summary of Jürgen Moltmann's *Theology of Hope*

IT IS SIGNIFICANT AND noteworthy that Jürgen Moltmann's theological formation was not shaped in a vacuum, nor exclusively in the context of academia. Jürgen Moltmann was a prisoner of war during World War II, from approximately 1945 through 1947. Adolf Hitler and Nazi Germany served as the political and cultural context, informing the social milieu of Moltmann as a young man. It was this reality that would inform *Theology of Hope*, in juxtaposition to the dire zeitgeist permeating Europe, in the wake of an estimated sixty million deaths resulting from the war. In addition, Jürgen Moltmann was influenced by the Marxist philosopher Ernst Bloch, as well as the thinking of Georg Hegel, for better or worse depending upon one's theological tendencies.

Jürgen Moltmann's *Theology of Hope* has a number of important themes that it focuses upon which are significant to understanding his theology. The fundamental themes of *Theology of Hope* are: hope, resurrection, eschatology, faith, and future.

Moltmann begins with his assertion that hope is a fundamental necessity for life itself. Life without hope is a dystopia for Moltmann. "Totally without hope one cannot live. To live without hope is to cease to live. Hell is hopelessness. It is not accident that above the entrance to Dante's hell is the inscription: Leave behind all hope, you who enter here."[1]

It is not surprising that Moltmann's experiences in World War II Germany would evolve into a major theological tenet in *Theology of Hope*. Hope is the most fundamental aspect of human existence; however, it is not a hope that is abstract for Moltmann or hope that is not grounded in something. That grounding for Moltmann leads into the future informed by potential. "For our knowledge and comprehension of reality, and our reflections on it, that means at least this: that in the medium of hope our theological concepts become not judgments which nail reality down to what it is, but anticipations which show reality its prospects and its future possibilities."[2]

In a *Theology of Hope*, Jürgen Moltmann demonstrates the interconnectedness of faith and resurrection. Christianity is able to give hope to the hopeless through the resurrection of Jesus the Christ. Christianity must first start with the resurrection of Christ and move forward from this moment in history. "Christianity stands or falls with the reality of the raising of Jesus from the dead by God. In the New Testament there is no faith that does not start a priori with the resurrection of Jesus."[3]

For Moltmann, in a *Theology of Hope*, resurrection is redefined or repurposed to lead us not so much into the past, however, but into the future. Moltmann challenges traditional theology and how resurrection is traditionally understood, as a past historic event that is complete and relegated to history. It is in the resurrection for Moltmann that the future finds hope for humanity. "The raising of Christ is then to be called 'historic,' not because it took place in the history to which other categories of some sort provide a key, but it is to be called historic because, by pointing the way for

---

1. Moltmann, *Theology of Hope*, 32.
2. Moltmann, *Theology of Hope*, 35.
3. Moltmann, *Theology of Hope*, 165.

future events, it makes history in which we can and must live. It is historic, because it discloses an eschatological future."[4]

Moltmann describes the event of the resurrection not as a morbid defeat of humanity through the triumph of evil and death; but that the suffering and death of Christ is paradoxical, a transvaluation, that which is counterintuitive and is the means through which humanity has life. "The raising of Christ is not merely a consolation to him in a life that is full of distress and doomed to die, but it is also God's contradiction of suffering and death, of humiliation and offense, and of the wickedness of evil."[5]

Eschatology for Moltmann in *Theology of Hope* challenges theologically to understand the eschaton not as confined to the end of things, not as the completion of human history, however, to synthesize the present into our eschatological thinking. Eschatology then is the radical change of the present. "From first to last, and not merely in the epilogue, Christianity is eschatology, is hope, transforming the present. The eschatological is not one element of Christianity, but it is the medium of Christian faith as such, the key in which everything in it is set, the glow that suffuses everything here in the dawn of an expected day."[6]

Assessment of Strengths and Weaknesses

Theology of Hope is vulnerable to criticism in certain theological circles because it is in conversation with Ernst Bloch, Georg Hegel, and Marxism. Writing in *Revisiting Moltmann's Theology of Hope* in the light of its renewed impact on emergent theology, Noel B. Woodbridge observes the following; "Moltmann was influenced by Marxism and the philosophies of Georg Hegel. . . . However, Hegel's ideas are philosophical and have not been proven in the real world. Moltmann took Hegel's ideas and created a Christian

---

4. Moltmann, *Theology of Hope*, 181.

5. Moltmann, *Theology of Hope*, 21.

6. Moltmann, *Theology of Hope*, 16.

alternative to Marxism (which is also based on Hegel's philosophy) that he called a theology of hope."[7]

This criticism is misguided because it intimates that philosophical ideas are always and necessarily antithetical to Christian systems of belief or theology. It is true that some ideas borrowed from philosophical ideas are hostile to Christian thought. Ideas, however, are conceptual to all of humanity and are not limited to parochial boundaries of religious thought, that is assuming one is not confined to the notion of revelation exclusively to Christians. Ideas or concepts which improve the human condition should be incorporated into Christian theological and ethical thought.

Jürgen Moltmann's futuristic theology is vulnerable to criticism of quietism if one is not careful to understand *Theology of Hope*. In communities of color this theological typology is often referred to as the religion of the oppressor or the oppressive class. A type of religion to placate communities into accepting their social conditions, and to anticipate better conditions in the next life. This type of theology when misunderstood was utilized by southern plantation owners to maintain order within the system of slavery.

It is here that Moltmann renders a strong refutation of the notion of quietism. "That is why faith, wherever it develops into hope, causes not rest but unrest, not patience but impatience. It does not calm the unquiet heart, but is itself this unquiet heart in man. Those who hope in Christ can no longer put up with reality as it is, but begin to suffer under it, to contradict it. Peace with God means conflict with the world . . . "[8]

The criticism that *Theology of Hope* is futuristic and does not give full autonomy to the person of God is a vulnerability to some. To these critics, Moltmann appears to have elements of process theology, to the extent that humanity has a role in aiding God in the rescuing of the creation. "According to the theology of hope proclaimed by Moltmann and his Emergent disciples, 'the truth will only be known with certainty in the future.' Therefore, this

7. Woodbridge, "Revisiting Moltmann's *Theology of Hope*," 110.

8. Moltmann, *Theology of Hope*, 21.

uncertainty results in the consequent heresies that 'God is recreating the world now with our help' and the world has a universally bright future with no pending, cataclysmic judgment."[9]

If we love God, and God's creation, then elements of Christian universalism are appealing as opposed to eternal damnation. Is it more Christian to hope for in the resurrection of Christ, the reconciliation of all creatures and not others? Critics of Moltmann here are selective in their biblical leanings. Perhaps the text in the Gospel of John could be applied. "And other sheep I have, which are not of this fold: them also I must bring, and they shall hear my voice; and there shall be one fold, and one shepherd" (John 10:16 KJV).

Relevance of Work

"Hundreds of Kodak's clicked all morning at the scene of the lynching. People in automobiles and carriages came from miles around to view the corpse dangling from the end of a rope. Picture cards photographers installed a portable printing plant at the bridge and reaped a harvest in selling the postcard showing a photograph of the lynched Negro."[10]

Such is the context and experience of African Americans in these United States; from slavery to Jim Crow, terrorism was the daily existence from circa 1619 and culminating in 1981 with the lynching of Michael Donald in Alabama. *Theology of Hope* provides a theology to all oppressed people that says there is a future in Christ, in the resurrection and in the eschaton, which offers hope beyond the present reality.

The kinship between Jürgen Moltmann and many of the liberation theologians and black theology theologians, though recently pushed back against by some theologians, is found in the transvaluation, dialectic, *mysterium tremendum* of salvific hope of all who suffer presently; in their marginalized experiences in

9. Woodbridge, "Revisiting Moltmann's *Theology of Hope*," 110.
10. Cone, *The Cross and the Lynching Tree*, 1.

the United States, Latin America, and other desperate locations around the world. That their present reality will yield to the hope found in the resurrection of Christ and the future in the eschatological hope.

Theology of Hope is a pedagogy of hope and praxis for the pulpit theologian, the seminary student, college and university religious studies, and the public square. At its best it is not assigned to oppressed people; however, people who are concerned about the plight of all of humanity.

CHAPTER 12

On W. E. B. Du Bois
and Double Consciousness

I. Introduction—Concept of Double Consciousness

THE DILEMMA OF AFRICAN Americans, living within the binary reality of being both African and American, is one which inherently possesses existential implications depending upon how African Americans have responded to this bifurcation. In Howard Thurman's *Jesus and the Disinherited*, in a chapter aptly titled "Deception," Thurman describes the dilemma of African Americans as captured in the quandary of all disinherited people. "The underprivileged may decide to juggle the various areas of compromise, on the assumption that the moral quality of compromise operates in an ascending-descending scale. According to this argument, not all issues are equal in significance nor in consequence . . . "[1]

The African American has too often been confronted with a *Sophie's Choice*, a type of cognitive dissonance, as it pertains to

1. Thurman, *Jesus and the Disinherited*, 66.

losing oneself and one's cultural identity, by fully integrating into the dominant culture, or conscientiously becoming a dissident and incurring the full wrath of the dominant culture. "All over the world there are millions of people who are condemned by the powerful in their society to live in ghettos. The choice seems to be the ghetto or suicide . . . there are great numbers of people who have decided to live, and to compromise on the matter of place and conditions."[2] One might metaphorically describe the social conditions of African Americans, the historical predicament, as a protracted ghetto. Being African in America is to be confronted with decisions on a daily basis that have existential consequences depending upon the response or responses given. It is this reality that has caused a decompensation in the psychological health and profile of African Americans.

W. E. B. Du Bois posits that the de facto dual citizenship of being black and American is inherently in a state of conflict. Having been inspired by the previous work of psychologists in the field of mental health, dealing with the malady of split personalities, Du Bois makes use of this imagery to describe the double consciousness of Africans in America and its resultant psychosis. " . . . The psychology idea of double consciousness further reinforced what Du Bois had emphasized as the genuinely alternative character of African American ideals. In the classic cases of double consciousness, the dual personalities were not just different from each other but were inevitably in opposition."[3] The occasion for the opposition of these competing realities of Africans in America, and those of European descent, would have catastrophic implications beginning in 1619 until present day.

Du Bois defines double consciousness as manifesting in a variety of ways. " . . . Du Bois used 'double consciousness' to refer to at least three different issues—including the first real power of white stereotypes in black life and thought and second the double consciousness created by the practical racism that excluded every

---

2. Thurman, *Jesus and the Disinherited*, 67.
3. Du Bois, *Souls of Black Folk*, 242.

black American from the mainstream of the society . . . "[4] The effects of double consciousness will have dire consequences for African American culture and institutions.

II. Historical Facets of Double Consciousness in African American Culture and Institutions

It is no small wonder that ground zero for the advancement of the Negro would play out in the context of education, with the epicenter being none other than the classroom. Historically, because of the liberating power of education, every measure was taken to prohibit access to education for persons of color. Miguel A. De La Torre writing in *Doing Christian Ethics from the Margins*, identifies the significance of the classroom and its contributing to the double consciousness effect for black people. "The (class) room is appropriately named, for it is indeed a room of class—a room where students learn the class they belong to and the power and privilege that comes with that class . . . they will have certain opportunities that are denied to those of lower economic classes."[5]

The debilitating effect of illiteracy, and its resulting contribution to the double consciousness of the Negro, has been a historic aspect of the struggle between black people and white people. This struggle began soon after the arrival of Africans on the shores of this country. Heather Andrea Williams, in an article titled "SELF-TAUGHT" describes the penalty for teaching enslaved blacks to read. "Most White Southern slaveholders were adamantly opposed to the education of their slaves because they feared an educated slave population would threaten their authority. Williams documents a series of statues that criminalized any person who taught slaves or supported their efforts to teach themselves."[6] The legacy of illiteracy still affects the black community in contemporary society. Jean Jacques Rousseau, writing in *Rousseau's The Social*

---

4. Du Bois, *Souls of Black Folk*, 238.

5 De La Torre, *Christian Ethics from the Margins*, xi.

6. D. S., "Review of *SELF-TAUGHT*," para. 2.

Contract, states that eventually persons confined to a certain condition, will accept his or her condition without attempting to improve upon their circumstances. "Slaves lose everything in their chains, even the desire of escaping from them . . . "[7]

Tragically, Rousseau's commentary has proven accurate for far too many within oppressed communities, who have become victims of what experts in race relations refer to as *internalized racial oppression.* This phenomenon accounts in part for the violence in many urban black communities such as Detroit, Baltimore, and other urban centers.

Arguably, the fractured black family, rates of incarceration, and other pathologies can be traced to the origin of black double consciousness in America, and the prolonged state of deprivation historically imposed upon the race.

Plessy v. Ferguson. Separate but equal. In 1896, the United States Supreme Court ruled that it was legal for public entities in the United States to legally impose segregation laws, thereby restricting *Negroes* access to public facilities. The public segregation of black people and white people further exasperated the sense of second class citizenry among the Negro population, deepening the double consciousness effect. The Reverend Dr. Martin Luther King Jr. chronicled the effect of segregation and the resulting double consciousness in "Letter From Birmingham City Jail" in 1963, as he articulated the impact of segregation upon his own family. " . . . Explain to your six-year old daughter why she can't go to the public amusement park . . . and see the depressing clouds of inferiority begin to form in her little mental sky, and see her begin to distort her little personality."[8] Public facilities that were segregated were never actually equal.

It is a matter of both public and private debate as to the legacy of segregation in the United States. As Dr. King referenced, segregation had a debilitating effect upon the psychology of the black community, and no well informed observer would dispute this

7. Rousseau, *The Social Contract*, 6.
8. King Jr., *A Testament of Hope*, 292–93.

fact. What is less clear is the legacy that was established as a result of segregation.

Some of the most esteemed black institutions emerged out of segregation in America. In 1876 the Meharry Medical College was founded in Nashville, Tennessee. In Oklahoma, *black Wall Street* witnessed the flourishing of black businesses until 1921 when angry white mobs destroyed the city during riots. During World War II, due to segregation in the United States military, separate units emerged showcasing the prowess of the black military genius such as the *Tuskegee Airmen*. From circa 1866 through 1951 the *Buffalo Soldiers* served with distinction as the 25th Infantry Regiment. In 1867, Howard University was founded as an institution of higher education for the education and training of the *Negro*. In 1861, Morehouse College was founded boasting some of the greatest leaders as its presidents, such as Dr. Benjamin E. Mays. Some scholars make the argument that with integration came what is known as *Brain Drain*, the migration of black intellectualism to white centered institutions.

Nevertheless, the battle to combat the corrosive effects of double consciousness, and to ameliorate the schizophrenia of black life in America, received a decisive victory on May 17, 1954. In that year the Brown v. Board of Education decision was handed down by the United States Supreme Court, ruling that segregation in public education was unconstitutional. The Brown v. Board of Education, though slow to be fully enforced, was a watershed moment for black people and black history. What is often overshadowed is that the impetus of Brown v. Board of Education was the *black church*. The African Methodist Episcopal Church, founded by Richard Allen in 1816 in Philadelphia, has an illustrious history in the annals of civil rights for persons of color in the United States.

The Reverend Oliver Brown, an African Methodist Episcopal pastor, wanted to enroll his daughter Linda Brown in the nearest school to their home. Because of segregation the family had to incur a circuitous route to the nearest school for black children. "Brown, an African Methodist Episcopal Church pastor . . . wanted his daughter to be allowed to enroll in the all-white elementary school—not because the all-white school was superior to the all-black elementary school she attended two miles away—but because it was a matter of principle."[9]

In December of 1955, only a year after Brown v. Board of Education, another African Methodist Episcopal Church member was involved with a historic moment in American history. Rosa Parks, through quiet dignity and steely grace, would continue the trajectory of momentum initiated by Reverend Oliver Brown. The *black church* has been an indispensable catalyst in mitigating the effects of double consciousness in the psychology of the African American community.

III. Double Consciousness Redux: Ta-Nehisi Coates' "Letter to My Son"

Ta-Nehisi Coates, writing in *The Atlantic* in 2015 published an article titled "Letter to My Son." In this letter, Coates expresses many of the concerns of which Du Bois addressed in his double consciousness, published in *The Souls of Black Folk* in 1903 over a century later. "Now, the heirs of slaveholders could never directly acknowledge our beauty or recon with its power. And so the beauty of the black body was never celebrated in the movies, on television shows, or in the textbooks I'd see as a child."[10] In this literary work Coates challenges the assertion that the *American Dream* will be realized with the passage of time. As a millennial, it is quite troubling in Coates' view, that the state of the union for black people in America is perceived as dire as at any time in American history. To make his argument, Coates recalls the litany of names of those victims killed by the police; Tamir Rice, Eric Garner, Michael Brown, and others all killed for their *black bodies* as Coates refers to it. "And you know now, if you did not before, that the police departments of your country have been endowed

9. Brown, "The determined father who took Linda Brown," para. 4.

10. Coates, "Letter to My Son," para. 21.

with the authority to destroy your body . . . sell cigarettes without the proper authority and your body can be destroyed."[11]

IV. Ecumenical Religious Practices—Nicholas Wolterstorff

How might ecumenism play a role in negating double consciousness and the debilitating effects of double consciousness? Political theologian Nicholas Wolterstorff emphasizes the role of reconciliation as a move toward the *beloved community*. Writing in *Acting Liturgically: Philosophical Reflections On Religious Practice*, Wolterstorff specifies reconciliation in his chapter, "Christ-like friendship in love in the assemblies includes reconciliation." "Both Jesus and Didache suggests that the reconciliation that is to prevail in the assemblies is to be brought about in advance . . . there is also opportunity within liturgical enactments for alienated participants to become reconciled by the combination of repentance and forgiveness."[12]

Repentance through individual acts of contrition, as well as the penitence of social institutions for their role in slavery and Jim Crow, as was the case of Princeton Theological Seminary making reparations. As well, the ability to genuinely live into forgiveness by those who are heirs of the legacy of racism; to construct opportunities to realize this process, perhaps a type of *truth & reconciliation* modeled after the South Africa paradigm.

It is a type of transvaluation that through Christianity, Africans in America were decimated, and America weaponized religion to engage a genocide against them; that perhaps through Christianity and ecumenism African Americans and white America may be reconciled.

---

11. Coates, "Letter to My Son," para. 6.
12. Wolterstorff, *Acting Liturgically*, 260.

Author's Note

It is remarkable that African Americans, the descendants of slaves, embrace Christianity at all. The imagination that is necessary to parse biblical text and find within it a theology that speaks to their context, is a testimony to their will to survive in a hostile land. Black religion embraces the cross and the narrative of Jesus as Savior, both theologically and culturally. But this does not suggest that African Americans have not historically, and do not now, struggle with the reconciliation of the cross and black life and suffering. African Americans are well aware of the shared relationship of Christianity with the white oppressors of history. The religion that helped African Americans to survive is the religion that was instrumental in their near genocide.

—Dr. Larry Covin
*Thirteen Turns: A Theology Resurrected From
the Gallows of Jim Crow Christianity*

Author's Note

Dr. Larry Covin is the Systematic Theologian-Religion Scholar at Trinity UCC Church in York, Pennsylvania. He earned the Bachelor of Science degree from Albany State University, Master of Divinity degree from the Interdenominational Theological Center, Doctor of Ministry degree from the Lancaster Theological Seminary, and postdoctoral ThM degree from the Princeton Theological Seminary.

Dr. Covin has served as adjunct professor at Morgan State University, Howard Community College, University of Baltimore, Lutheran Theological Seminary, Lancaster Theological Seminary, and the Schaefer Center for Public Policy.

Bibliography

Achebe, Chinua. *Things Fall Apart*. Portsmouth, NH: Heinemann, 1994.

"'A Chosen Exile': Black People Passing in White America." Karen Bates Grigsby. *All Things Considered*. Aired October 7, 2014, on NPR. Radio.

Barnett, Victoria J. *"After Ten Years": Dietrich Bonhoeffer and Our Times*. Minneapolis: Fortress, 2017.

Bentham, Jeremy. *Writings on the Poor Laws*. 2 vols. Edited by Michael Quinn. The Collected Works of Jeremy Bentham. Oxford: Oxford University Press, 2010.

Bonhoeffer, Dietrich. *The Bonhoeffer Reader*. Edited by Clifford Green and Michael P. DeJonge. Minneapolis: Fortress, 2013.

Brown, DeNeen L. "The determined father who took Linda Brown by the hand and made history." *The Washington Post*, May 27, 2018. https://www.washingtonpost.com/news/retropolis/wp/2018/03/27/the-determined-black-dad-who-took-linda-brown-by-the-hand-and-stepped-into-history/.

Brundage, Anthony. "The English Poor Law of 1834 And The Cohesion of Agricultural Society." *Agricultural History* 48, no. 3 (July 1974) 405–417.

Clark, Elaine. "Institutional and Legal Responses to Begging in Medieval England." *Social Science History* 26, no. 3 (Fall 2002) 447–473.

Coates, Ta-Nehisi. "Letter to My Son." *The Atlantic*, July 4, 2015. https://www.theatlantic.com/politics/archive/2015/07/tanehisi-coates-between-the-world-and-me/397619/.

Cohen, Andrew. "The Speech That Shocked Birmingham the Day After the Church Bombing." *The Atlantic,* September 13, 2013.

Cone, James H. *The Cross and the Lynching Tree*. Maryknoll, NY: Orbis, 2011.

De La Torre, Miguel A. *Doing Christian Ethics from the Margins*. Maryknoll, NY: Orbis, 2004.

Digby, Anne. "Malthus and Reform of the Poor Law." In *Malthus Past and Present*, edited by Jacques Dupaquier, 97–110. Population and Social Structure. London: Academic, 1983.

D. S. Review of *SELF-TAUGHT: African American Education in Slavery and Freedom*, by Heather Andrea Williams. *Harvard Educational Review* 77, no. 3 (2005).

Du Bois, W. E. B. *The Souls of Black Folk*. Edited by Henry Louis Gates Jr. and Terri Hume Oliver. Norton Critical Editions. New York: Norton, 1999.

Gates Jr., Louis Henry. "The New Negro and the Black Image: From Booker T. Washington to Alain Locke." Freedom's Story, TeacherServe. National Humanities Center. http://nationalhumanitiescenter.org/tserve/freedom/1917beyond/essays/newnegro.htm.

Geremek, Bronislaw. *Poverty: A History*. Translated by Agnieszka Kolakowska. Oxford: Blackwell, 1994.

Gibson, Katie. "Healthcare as a civil rights issue: New Research from Amitabh Chandra offers solutions to improve minority healthcare in the U.S." Harvard Kennedy School, June 8, 2017. https://www.hks.harvard.edu/research-insights/policy-topics/health/healthcare-civil-rights-issue.

Graham, Lawrence Otis. *Our Kind of People: Inside America's Black Upper Class*. New York: HarperCollins, 2009.

Grant II, Ernest Cleo. "Looking for Ancient African Religion? Try Christianity." *Christianity Today*, January 18, 2018. https://www.christianitytoday.com/ct/2018/january-web-only/urban-christianity-ancient-africa-apologetics.html.

Higginbotham, Peter. "The Workhouse in Berkshire." *Berkshire Family Historian*. www.berksfhs.org.uk/journal.

Hodgkin, Peter C., and Robert H. King, eds. *Readings in Christian Theology*. Minneapolis: Fortress, 1985.

Howard University. "Andrew Rankin Memorial Chapel: History And Legacy." https://chapel.howard.edu/about/history-and-legacy.

Ivimey, Joseph. *Memoir of William Fox, Esq., Founder of the Sunday-School Society: Comprising the History of the Origin and First Twenty Years of that Benevolent and Useful Institution—with the Correspondence on the Subject Between Wm. Fox, Esq., and Robert Raikes, Esq., of Gloucester, the Father of the Sunday-school System, and Other Distinguished Persons*. London: Paternoster Row, 1831.

Jaschik, Scott. "Closing Arguments in the Harvard Case." *Inside Higher Ed*, February 18, 2019. https://www.insidehighered.com/admissions/article/2019/02/18/critics-and-defenders-affirmative-action-submit-their-closing-briefs.

Kedourie, Elie. *Nationalism*. 4th ed. Malden, MA: Blackwell, 1993.

The King Center. "The King Philosophy." https://thekingcenter.org/king-philosophy/.

King Jr., Martin Luther. "Address at the Conclusion of the Selma to Montgomery March." Speech, Montgomery, AL, March 25, 1965, https://kinginstitute.stanford.edu/king-papers/documents/address-conclusion-selma-montgomery-march.

Bibliography

———. *A Testament of Hope: The Essential Writings and Speeches*. Edited by James M. Washington. San Francisco: HarperOne, 2003.

Kohler-Haussmann, Issa. *Misdemeanorland: Criminal Courts and Social Control in an Age of Broken Windows Policing*. Princeton: Princeton University Press, 2018.

Lebacqz, Karen. *Six Theories of Justice: Perspectives from Philosophical and Theological Ethics*. Minneapolis: Augsburg, 1986.

Lezama, Darryl. *From the Civil Rights Pioneers to the First African American President and Beyond: Forging a More Perfect Union by Eliminating Injustice, Racism, Poverty, and Violence*. Bloomington, IN: AuthorHouse, 2014.

Marable, Manning. "The Meaning of Faith in the Black Mind in Slavery." *Rocky Mountain Review of Language and Literature* 30, no. 4 (Autumn 1976) 248–64. https://www.jstor.org/stable/1347694?seq=1.

Markowitz, Eric. "Making Profits On The Captive Prison Market." *New Yorker*, September 4, 2016. https://www.newyorker.com/business/currency/making-profits-on-the-captive-prison-market.

Marripedia. "Effects of Religious Practice on Education." http://marripedia.org/effects_of_religious_practice_on_education.

Mays, Benjamin. "Benjamin Mays, Class of 1920, eulogy for the Rev. Martin Luther King Jr." Eulogy, Morehouse College, Atlanta, April 9, 1968. https://www.bates.edu/150-years/months/april/benjamin-mays-king-eulogy/.

McCormack, Bruce. "Locating Christian Faith on a Map of Religious Consciousness." Lecture, Princeton Theological Seminary, Princeton, NJ, February 4, 2019.

———. "The Origin of the Church: Election and the Communication of the Holy Spirit." Lecture, Princeton Theological Seminary, Princeton, NJ, February 18, 2019.

Mill, John Stuart. *Utilitarianism*. https://www.utilitarianism.com/mill1.htm.

Mitchell, Bruce. "Jazz: A Multicultural Phenomenon." *The Clearing House* 65, no. 4 (March–April 1992) 236–38.

Moltmann, Jürgen. *The Crucified God*. Minneapolis: Fortress, 2015.

———. *Theology of Hope*. Minneapolis: Fortress, 1993.

Niebuhr, Reinhold. *Moral Man And Immoral Society: A Study in Ethics and Politics*. Rev. ed. Louisville: Westminster John Knox, 2001.

———. *The Nature And Destiny of Man: A Christian Interpretation*. Vol. 2, *Human Destiny*. Louisville: Westminster John Knox, 1996.

Nietzsche, Friedrich. "Slave and Master Morality." In *Reading for Philosophical Inquiry: A Brief Introduction*, 1–12. https://philosophy.lander.edu/intro/articles/nietzsche-a.pdf.

Pew Research Center. "Religion and Education Around the World." December 13, 2016. https://www.pewforum.org/2016/12/13/religion-and-education-around-the-world/.

Pojman, Louis P., and Lewis Vaughn. *The Moral Life: An Introductory Reader in Ethics and Literature*. Oxford: Oxford University Press, 2007.

Price, Kim. "'Where Is The Fault?': The Starvation of Edward Cooper at the Isle of Wight Workhouse in 1877." *Social History of Medicine* 26, no. 1 (February 2013) 21–37.

Radcliffe, William. *Origin of the New System of Manufacture Commonly Called "power-loom Weaving," and the Purposes for which this System was Invented and Brought Into Use, Fully Explained in a Narrative, Containing William Radcliffe's Struggles Through Life to Remove the Cause which Has Brought this Country to Its Present Crisis.* Minneapolis: University of Minnesota Press, 1828.

Rawls, John. *A Theory of Justice.* Cambridge: Harvard University Press, 1971.

Richardson, Ruth. "Oliver Twist and the workhouse." *British Library*, May 15, 2014. https://www.bl.uk/romantics-and-victorians/articles/oliver-twist-and-the-workhouse.

Rousseau, Jean-Jacques. *Discourse on Inequality.* Translated by Franklin Philip. Oxford World's Classics. New York: Oxford University Press, 2009.

———. *The Social Contract.* Translated by Christopher Betts. Oxford World's Classics. New York: Oxford University Press, 1999.

Schleiermacher, Friedrich. *The Christian Faith.* New York: Harper & Row, 1963.

———. *On Religion: Speeches to its Cultured Despisers.* Cambridge Texts in the History of Philosophy. Cambridge: Cambridge University Press, 1988.

Sellin, J. Thorsten. *Slavery and the Penal System.* Classics of Law & Society. New Orleans: Quid Pro, 2016.

Slade, Rachel. "Is There Such a Thing as 'Good' Prison Design?" *Architectural Digest*, April 30, 2018. https://www.architecturaldigest.com/story/is-there-such-a-thing-as-good-prison-design.

Smith, Leonard. "Lunatic Asylum in the Workhouse: St. Peter's Hospital, Bristol, 1698–1861." *Medical History* 61, vol. 2 (April 2017) 225–45.

Sowell, Thomas. *Wealth, Poverty and Politics: An International Perspective.* New York: Basic, 2016.

Soylu, Erdinc, et al. "Vivien Theodore Thomas (1910–1985): An African-American Laboratory Technician Who Went On To Become An Innovator In Cardiac Surgery." *Journal of Medical Biography* 25, no. 2 (August 2015).

Thurman, Howard. *The Creative Encounter: An Interpretation of Religion and the Social Witness.* Richmond, IN: Friends United, 1972.

———. *Jesus and the Disinherited.* Nashville: Abingdon, 1949.

Tietz, Christiane. *Theologian of Resistance: The Life and Thought of Dietrich Bonhoeffer.* Translated by Victoria J. Barnett. Minneapolis: Fortress, 2016.

Twain, Mark. "The United States of Lyncherdom." http://people.virginia.edu/~sfr/enam482e/lyncherdom.html.

US Department of Justice. Office of Justice Programs. Bureau of Justice Statistics. *Special Report: Education and Correctional Populations*, by Caroline Wolf Harlow. NCJ 195670, January 2003.

Wagner, Terry. "America's Civil Rights Revolution—Three Documentaries About Emmett Till's Murder In Mississippi (1955)." *Historical Journal of Film, Radio and Television* 30, no. 2 (June 2010) 187–201.

White, Thomas. "What Did Hanna Arendt Really Mean by The Banality of Evil?" *Aeon*, April 23, 2018. https://aeon.co/ideas/what-did-hannah-arendt-really-mean-by-the-banality-of-evil.

Wiesel, Elie. *Night*. Translated by Marion Wiesel. New York: Hill & Wang, 2006.

Wolterstorff, Nicholas. *Acting Liturgically: Philosophical Reflections On Religious Practice*. Oxford: Oxford University Press, 2018.

———. *Educating for Shalom: Essays on Christian Higher Education*. Edited by Clarence W. Joldersma and Gloria Goris Stronks. Grand Rapids: Erdmans, 2004.

———. *Journey Toward Justice: Personal Encounters In The Global South*. Turning South: Christian Scholars in an Age of World Christianity. Grand Rapids: Baker Academic, 2013.

Woodson, Carter Godwin. *The Mis-Education of the Negro*. Trenton, NJ: Africa World, 1990.

Woodbridge, Noel. "Revisiting Moltmann's *Theology of Hope* in the light of its renewed impact on emergent theology." *Conspectus: The Journal of the South African Theological Seminary* 9, no. 3 (March 2010) 106–13.

Index

Index

CPSIA information can be obtained
at www.ICGtesting.com
Printed in the USA
LVHW010149180621
690501LV00014B/1507